Grace over Guilt

by Armando Perez

Cover Artwork // Simon Lee and Anne Nygard

To start this book off with a catchphrase or a one-liner of encouragement is not where I want to begin. I have no pre-meditation of fluffed up words to draw readers in. I could have easily opened this book with one of the many testimonies of horrible things I have done... like the story of illegally transporting Mexicans across the border when I was 22 years old or the one of how I almost killed a man in a drug deal gone bad. But I rather not put a spotlight on the dark moments of my life.

That is who I used to be, not who I am today.

Too often we glorify the places we have been and put little enthusiasm into where we are going.

It is common to hear stories of people's lives being transformed from darkness to light. Praise God for salvation, but I want to be careful to not put the emphasis of my personal testimony on the bad parts rather than the good part of the story, which is the saving grace of Jesus.

"If we remain focused on the struggles, the freedom from bondage becomes peripheral."

Being in bondage can feel like a caged animal looking for an escape route. When the soul feels trapped with no way out, most people's emotions turn inward to guilt and condemnation. Excuses and creative justifications flood the mind with lies and suddenly it can become a blame game for the internal struggle they are dealing with. Have you ever heard someone blame something or someone from their past for their problems? What about blaming God for their struggle? Or maybe you have heard someone ask, "Why is God allowing this to happen?"

> The thief does not come except to steal, and to kill, and to destroy. I have come that they may have life, and that they may have it more abundantly. John 10:10 – NKJV

In John, Jesus makes it clear that He came so that humanity can have an abundant life. It is the thief who steals, kills, and destroys... this thief is DECEPTION. It steals your joy, it kills your identity, and it destroys your life. There have been lies attacking the identity of our human race since the beginning of creation. The devil used deception to trick God's first man and woman into disobeying God. In good faith I can assure you; God is not at fault for our problems. Then who can we say is responsible?

Is it us?

Is it the devil?

We do not need to justify our problems. Justification for darkness is simply agreeing with darkness. If we justify reasons of unprincipled moral, it creates the false conclusion that we will always have to deal with the struggle of failure. That is not true. The Spirit of Christ empowers us to be free, and the Bible tells us that he who is free is free indeed. That word indeed means 'to be sure of,' or 'for certain.'

It is the lack of knowledge that takes away freedom's certainty. Not knowing what freedom looks like is an open playground for the enemy. If we are not careful, even as born-again Christians, instead of healing from guilt, shame, and condemnation; we might create a hiding place for all our junk. Rather than admitting our problems and giving them to God, we might stuff them deep down behind a locked door in our hearts and pretend everything is going great in our lives.

"The snake of deception slithers its way into a man's broken self-esteem, and it thrusts the soul into isolation."

Imagine this, you are sitting in a room and every person present is addressing their addictions and painful regrets. When you get to the last person in the room, you start judging each other based on a scale of whose life story was the worst. You agree with 'their struggles' to make 'your struggles' common amongst yourselves. Deception sets in and tells you that you are no different, and the things you are dealing with will always be a struggle. The sneaky little voice of deception tells you no one needs to know what you are going through, there is no hope, and this is how your life is always going to be. You do not want to be seen as weak and incapable, so you stay silent. You tell yourself that it is normal to have secrets and then you hide behind the made-up excuse that people will always have their struggles.

You have now taken the role of 'a struggling struggler' that is trying to do their best...

And before you even realize it, deception convinces you that you will never be free. or worse yet you will never be forgiven.

If we focus on the negative things in our lives, we can surely expect to manifest a more negative perspective in all areas. For example, we will see, think, and respond negatively.

But focusing on the positive can create a different life altogether.

Picture the day you received your salvation. God's grace is so remarkable, it washes us clean of our sinful nature. In that first saving moment, you received the redemptive freedom of God, but after time passes from the day of salvation, deception sneaks in and will try to convince you that the grace you received for free now has a price tag attached to it. You walk around feeling it is now up to you to make sure you qualify for God's grace again. Deception tells you that the Christian life gets harder as time goes on. It makes you feel unworthy of God's goodness, and most people began to lose hope in themselves and their faith.

"If you didn't know you were forgiven, you'd spend the rest of your life looking for it."

I have met people who live their Christian life in deception with feelings of "just trying to get by." Deception exhausts the believer with worry, and it makes them feel disqualified from righteousness by considering their works to now be their only accessible grace.

It creates a belief system of – 'if we do good, we get good and if we do bad, we get bad.'

Does that sound familiar?

Yet, if this were true, how is it any different from the view of an unbeliever? Even those who say they do not believe in God will agree to believe that if you do good, you will get good... That is not Jesus, that's Karma (derived from eastern world religions).

A repentant heart is not only saying "I'm sorry" to get a free pass. Someone who repents for all the sinful things they have done will understand that it is more than just words, it requires action. In my personal journey, there have been times that I needed to be reminded of God's goodness and grace, and to remember that I have truly been forgiven by Him once and for all.

In this book I am going to talk about the power of God's grace over the bondage of guilt, and how His love pertains to the life of the born-again believer in Jesus Christ.

I hope that this read will breathe the spirit of revelation over your life and that it will help lead you out of the repetitive actions of condemnation and into the open fields of freedom that Jesus paid so heavy a price for you to experience... I welcome you to what I call Grace over Guilt.

Chapter One – Acceptance Over Love

One morning as I was getting ready for work, I had a vision. I saw the word 'ACCEPTED' flash across my eyes. I have had moments of these type of visions before, yet it may be new to some that are reading this book, so I will explain.

I saw a visual image that suddenly appeared in front of me. It was an old piece of paper with the word ACCEPTED written across the center ruling. I was standing in my bathroom with a toothbrush in my hand and barely awake. The vision happened quickly. I did not see a host of heavenly angels singing or a burning bush like Moses in the desert, but I did see the word on paper. I knew the Spirit of the Lord was saying something. Just as quickly as the image had appeared before my eyes, it disappeared.

As I continued to brush my teeth, I began to think about what the word ACCEPTED had to do with my day... or week... or even my entire life? And then in my heart and in my mind, I could feel God was speaking to me, it was like He was whispering into my ear...

"My people are replacing love with acceptance."

It hit me like a tidal wave, and the revelation of His words began to pour forth! I started seeing moments that we as God's people have replaced real and genuine love with acceptance.

I realized that there are teachings in the church which have created this idea that the acceptance of people is enough.

Acceptance is good, but if we fail to love, uplift, and help others – what is benefited by acceptance alone? We are supposed to exemplify the love of Jesus, and not sit back and watch as people around us experience hardship.

Could it be true? Have we as God's people stopped loving our neighbors to a point that if we see them drowning in defeat, we let them suffer and tell them we will see them again next week at church? Have we turned away from love and accountability and replaced the commandment of Jesus? Is merely accepting one another enough?

And if all this is true, how do we turn back to love?

This all stems from a place of understanding the genuine love of God. And to know God's love, we first must acknowledge His grace.

It is easy to love others when we feel like they have been good to us, or because we want something from them. But often people have a challenging time loving without expectations. And an even harder thing to do is learning to love themselves… forgive themselves… confront and release themselves… and most importantly find themselves.

There is something about loving ourselves that Jesus wants us to see. He thought it to be of such importance, that He himself was willing to come down and show us what love really looks like.

God does not only accept us, but He also loves us! What a beautiful picture of love, that He became our sacrifice, so that we could be free! In return, He asked that we extend that love to others. But to fully grasp His love and to love others, we must be subjected to a major heart change.

God's grace does not save us to be able to sin and get away with it. It empowers you to walk out what God has called you to.

It is false to believe that God's grace keeps us from having to do what is right. It is true that His grace covers us, but it cost God everything to extend the highest magnitude of His love.

"Grace without change is a perversion of the grace of God!"

What I am about to say is the paragraph God put in my heart when I first produced the title of this book,

"People have a problem with themselves. They exclude their own type and feel who they want to be is unobtainable... They believe the lies that they are ugly, weak, worthless, useless – and live in guilt and shame. Only Jesus can see through the mess to bring to light who you really are. His blood washes away the labels and lies over us. And His love speaks a better word. That is His grace! It empowers you to become who you really are!"

I grew up in church but knew religion under the doctrine of performance and doing what I believed was acceptable in God's eyes. A religious seed was planted in my mind and watered over time by man's actions towards what I witnessed them do and not do. This picture of legal morality is exactly what the law looked like before Jesus came to fulfill what man could not do. As a young eager Christian, it was easy to place someone on a pedestal who I thought had it all together and to discredit myself because of all the terrible things I had done in my lifetime. This was a horrible cycle that took me over 30 years to break.

I share with you one of my favorite quotes:

"Do you believe that the God of Jesus loves you beyond worthiness and unworthiness, beyond fidelity and infidelity - that he loves you in the morning sun and in the evening rain - that he loves you when your intellect denies it, your emotions refuse it, your whole being rejects it? Do you believe that God loves without condition or reservation and loves you this moment as you are and not as you should be?" - Brennan Manning

This is the powerful message of the gospel that has captivated the hearts of the lost, the hungry, and the dying for thousands of years. That the creator of the world and everything in it – would somehow look through all the dark mess of your being and pierce through space, time, and matter. That He in all His infinite glory would not waste another second of another day to let you be driven further into the abyss of darkness, but that He sent His only son to redeem you from the curse of sickness, death, and the grave. And if you choose to receive it today – your sins will be forgiven forever, and you will be made right with Him eternally.

The only thing that stands in the way of receiving this free gift is a simple response…
Will you believe it? And will you receive it?

Chapter Two – WDJD? What Did Jesus Do?

In scripture, we understand that the Son of God came so that humanity would be saved and redeemed from the curse of sin and death. You can find good Easter Sunday sermons or teachings that will tell you about God's sacrifice to send His only son to die on the cross at Calvary 2000 + years ago… but how is that relevant for today?

I am glad you asked!

Let us start with what He accomplished on the cross…

For years, the law given by God needed a blood sacrifice to be an atonement, so that what was not right could be made right. The blood of bulls and goats was shed as a sacrifice, so that the children of God would be forgiven for their sins. This was a repetitive ceremony and the foreshadowing of another blood sacrifice that was to come. When God was no longer pleased with the blood of animals, the innocent blood of Jesus Christ was shed to be the final atonement for our sins. This is what was accomplished at Calvary.

Now let us talk about what Jesus' accomplished while He was here on the earth…

We know through scripture that Jesus fulfilled two things certain of the promised Messiah.

Number one, He fulfilled the law. Number two, He fulfilled the prophecies of the prophets of God. He was the fulfillment of God's perfect plan all along.

It started in the garden with God creating man in His own likeness. He named the man Adam, and He named Adam's wife Eve. One day they disobeyed God, and their disobedience created condemnation which kept them from repenting and asking for forgiveness. Instead, they chose to blame others for their actions. First Adam blamed Eve, then Eve blamed the serpent.

This made God angry, but God was angry at sin, not at Adam and Eve. Every day God would show up for a meeting with Adam, and the day Adam disobeyed God was no different. I will speak more about this in a chapter I have titled 'The Grounded Theory,' but for now I just want to make it clear that God was not angry at His creation.

The enemy is cunning, and he has been doing an excellent job for thousands of years at making people feel rejected, unworthy, and hopeless. He comes in through a devious plan to bring shame to you first, and then makes a subtle engagement for you to accept failure or relinquish your rights of acceptance from God and move you into not feeling like a good son or daughter.

In Romans, we understand that it was one man's decision to disobey God that created sin for the entire world. But because of Jesus, it was also one man's decision to obey God that created salvation for the entire world.

This was the fulfillment of why Jesus the son of God came off His heavenly throne to redeem a people who could not redeem themselves.

There were 10 original laws given to Moses on Mt. Sinai. These instructions were given to Moses by God to be a blueprint of what was acceptable and not acceptable. If the blueprint was offensive, it was because the person feeling the offense was not willing to accept what a Godly life should look like. It was a model for righteousness.

After many years those 10 commandments became 613 Jewish commandments through trial, error, and continual revelation from God through His chosen people. This made the road to holiness hard to keep. This is where the world lived for centuries. People were judged and outcast for their sins and left in the wilderness of their own struggles.

Unfortunately, this is a problem that still exists today. The more we feel abandoned and useless, the more the devil will slip in the claws of guilt, rejection, abandonment, and death.

God chose a group of people to oversee the law and make sure that all were following its order. These men would eventually see themselves as being of a higher status than anyone who did not know the law, and they opposed those who did not follow it. This created a spiritual hierarchy that in return left the people feeling unworthy and less accepted. It enhanced the attention of sin rather than the attention of Holiness.

For decades, the act to fulfill the law was the key to life of the descendants of Abraham and God's chosen people. There were arguments and judgements made against those who were not of the same blood line, and many people were rejected.

Doesn't this resemble the same type of religious rejection and conflict over indifferences that we see in the church today?

When Christ the Messiah came, He fulfilled every law required to live a holy life. God empowered Him to actively withdraw from every temptation, and He conquered the devil's schemes against humanity. Because of His obedience, He was the perfect human. He was spotless, without blame and without sin. This made Him the perfect sacrifice and the final atonement for all the world's sins.... past, present, and future! Amen!

Now let us look at the prophecies...

Jesus fulfilled over 300 prophecies of the Old Testament. It was the prophetic words of God's chosen spokespeople like the prophet Isaiah in 740 B.C. that proclaimed a coming savior and king who would one day rule over every nation of the world. Every prophetic declaration and word given by God was released to His people through mighty prophets that carried a bold anointing to shift kingdoms and nations. The coming Messiah was the focal point for many years for the people of Israel. They were living in conviction with the hopes of a coming king who would one day put an end to poverty, slavery, and the madness of the world.

At the time and presentation of the arrival of Jesus, the Jewish people thought that He was going to take rank and arms as a powerful army general to topple the forces of the Roman empire and all those that were a threat to the children of God. They had heard stories and witnessed powerful moves of God that canceled out missions of their enemies, like the Egyptian soldiers at the Red Sea and the Philistines at Ellah Valley. It would only make since that a Savior King would come to crush the enemy with a sword and shield... yet this was not the plan of God.

It was very precise that Jesus would come and fulfill all the words of these prophets. Even today we can be amazed at the precision and accuracy of the fulfillment of these foretold words.

Since the beginning God's word has always remained true!

It never falters, it never waivers, it never fades away, and it never dies.

Chapter Three - Love God, Love Your Neighbor, and Love Yourself

Matthew 22:37-39 NASB - And He said to him, "'You shall love the Lord your God with all your heart, and with all your soul, and with all your mind.' This is the great and foremost commandment. The second is like it, 'You shall love your neighbor as yourself.'

These are the words of Jesus. He was God's son in the flesh, sent to redeem humanity and fulfill the law. He in return gave us two commandments rather than the 613 no one was able to successfully keep. If you read further, verse 40 says, *"Upon these two commandments hang the whole Law and the Prophets."*

Why would Jesus say that these two commandments out of 613 hang the whole law and the prophets?

He explains that if a heart is set in true adoration, then all the other laws are effortless due to the overwhelming love that God has given us.

Let me simplify what I just said... If your heart is in love with God, you will only want what He wants. This cancels out "trying" and leaves you in a place of willing surrender to Him. The problem I have seen in most people, is in their Christian walk they often become drained. Their heart becomes hardened, they lose enjoyment in their relationship, and they come to a place they do not "feel" God or "hear" God.

We have been given an outline of the perfect relationship by the Father and His Son. And this is the very thing that Jesus said we must do. He erased the hundreds of 'do's and don'ts,' and in return gave us a small list.

The first being to love God.

Jesus said, "love the Lord your God with all your heart." Your heart primarily is the thing that drives you each day. It not only pumps physical blood but is the chamber of your affections attached to your soul. It is where your belief system is settled, and it creates the atmosphere for your mind to use its imagination.

Then He said, "love with all your soul'. Your soul is the very thing that makes you distinct from every other creature and being. It is who you are. I once heard it said that we are a living soul that owns a physical body rather than a physical body that owns a soul. We are the groundwork of God here on the earth. The deepest and innermost part of your person is your soul, and it belongs only to you. God chooses to not invade your soul but allows it to be your own place of free will and choice. Each time you make a choice, you make a memory. And those memories are etched into your soul. Every experience is carved into your remembrance. This incorporates a sense of decisive direction based on the experiential situations of your life. Your soul is like your own personal handwritten journal. Once you write in the pages of this journal it is hard to erase the ink. Sometimes we are left with torn pages and messed up lines, but what is fascinating about the soul is that it can be renewed.

How can it be renewed?

The answer is by the renewing of the mind.

Romans 12:2 ESV - "Do not be conformed to this world, but be transformed by the renewal of your mind, that by testing you may discern what is the will of God, what is good and acceptable and perfect."

When we allow God to work in us, it changes the way we see our circumstances. He helps us discern what He wants, rather than what we think we need. When spiritual growth takes root, it creates a will in us that only desires the things that are good for us, and not the things that tear us down. We must permit the truth of God's word to become alive and active in us. It creates a resting place for our soul. It is a place of peace and clarity that is non-negotiable with the chaos of the world. We must learn to run into the arms of a loving Father because His love is our only assured security.

To love God with all your soul means to allow Him to move in and make the changes inside of you that He wants. When we die to ourselves, He truly lives through us. He always knows what is best, and our surrender to Him is what He desires.

"It is the love of our King that He would choose to lay down His own life to grant us His righteousness."

In His commandment, Jesus also tells us, "Love with all your mind." Our minds are filled with memories and thoughts derived from our individual experiences. The way we grew up and things we have experienced often are what leads our thinking. It has a major effect on the way we listen and the way we assume. If we are not careful to follow God's truth, then by default we will always make decisions and act out according to our own logic. Once we become a new creation in Christ and we are pursuing God's will, it is vital that we seek guidance from the Holy Spirit and remain in the truth of our identity. It is our responsibility to keep our faith in Him and turn away from the things of the past. We must always believe we are who He says we are.

Let me be clear, turning away does NOT mean running away.

There are millions of positive teachings, bestselling books, and motivational speeches adapted from subjective experiences that help educate us in the growth process of life.

In Peter Scazzero's book, Emotionally Healthy Spirituality, he says, *"It's easy to assume that your past is simply dead and gone, having no impact on you or what you're looking to do in the future. But assuming is harmful to your emotions and spiritual health."*

If we sweep all our past traumas and abuse under a rug and pretend it never affects us again, it easily becomes a one-man management system forcing us to carry the burden of performance to feel free. This is inclusive of the hope of containing all the comfort we need to stay stable enough to "do right" and not fall into temptation or sin again. The truth is most people are drug through the mud most of their lives to the extent that they do not know what it feels like to be clean.

Aren't you glad that the blood of Jesus makes us clean?

His sacrifice and finished work can now give you peace of mind knowing that the enemy's bondage, both past and present, has lost the battle to keep you from becoming a new creation! Praise Him!

When Jesus said love God with all your mind, He was simply saying keep your focus on the Father always. In every circumstance and in every situation keep your mind stayed on Him. This is the key to a life that lives in peace. Through every happy moment, every hurting moment, every victory, and every battle against your giants… keep your eyes on Jesus. This is the only way to stay at peace.

The second commandment says, "love your neighbor as yourself."
Recently, I sat with a man who had made poor life choices. He belonged to a wealthy family and had a problem-free childhood. But as an adult he wandered off into sexual perversion and eventually was exposed in a scandal that rocked his family and hometown to the core. Not long after

the news spread of what happened, his counselor reached out to me, to meet with him.

My first reaction was… Grace over Guilt.

I remembered the story of the woman caught in adultery and thrown at the feet of Jesus. Jesus did not ask for details; He was not interested in hearing any reason. He simply forgave her and affirmed to her that she was free from shame and guilt. In likeness, I did not know the details of this man's story or all that had taken place, I had no interest in hearing reason. I was not there to point my finger at him and remind him of all the things he had done wrong. Rather, I was to sit with him and point out all the things that Jesus the savior of the world had done right. We began meeting once a week.

One morning as I sat at this man's table, the Holy Spirit came over me and out of my mouth came something that to this day I am still finding revelation in.

I looked at this man and said, *"I will not sit here in your home and question if you love God."*

I believe he did… After the mistakes he made, he had gone into a deep repentance, and I had witnessed the changes that were happening in his heart.

Then I said, *"And I'm not going to sit here at your table and ask if you love others."*

I can attest that his heart had been softened, and he was now eager to learn how to love like Jesus.

And then out of my mouth came, *"But, I will sit here and ask you… Do you love yourself?"*

That was it! I realized that God wants us to become three things and not just the two we glance over in Jesus' statement...

"Love God, love your neighbor, and love yourself."

It is easy to understand we need to forgive others and to love God, but even so, it is equally important that we love ourselves, forgive ourselves, and believe the best about ourselves. This was a life-altering realization for me, and I pray that it becomes that way for you as well. I pray that you will see that you can give your guilt, shame, and condemnation to the Father and never look back to place accusation on yourself. He will work out all things for good to them that love Him.

Brennan Manning says, "Real freedom is freedom from the opinions of others. Above all, freedom from your opinions about yourself."

I have done horrible things in my past. I have hurt people, lied, stolen, and cheated. 20 years of my life I was caught up in sin and self-pleasure. Then I came to the end of myself and cried out for God to save me... and He did. But because I had lived such a terrible way before, I wanted to do my best to make sure I would stay on God's good side. I slipped into a works mentality. I had this idea that I needed to perform and produce to be fulfilled and to be continually accepted, and eventually I found myself in a struggle of trying to 'do good' and not fail.

I had gone from the free gift of salvation to all work and no rest. It started to weigh me down with the burden of continual pressure. For years, I felt a downward spiral of worry and stress. I put so much expectation on myself for so long that I had escaped the bondage of sin and fell right into the bondage of religion.

It was not until I found the truth of God's grace that I understood there were no expectations to live up to. This is the essence of God's grace over all our lives. It is the immeasurable power of God's goodness and His love for us that supersedes all our mess ups and failures. It is His goodness that leads people to repentance and to salvation.

When I started making Jesus the priority of my accountability, not from works but from a place of love, I started seeing changes in my character, in my feelings, and my life. It seemed like all the years of trying so hard slipped right out the window and all I had left was a deep desire to be in the same room with Jesus. I had fallen out of the world and in love with the one that had given it all for me. My perspective of the challenges in my life changed. I no longer saw them as something I was destined to struggle with. The assurance and peace of God allowed me to decide how I would let those things to affect me. I was empowered by His love for me, and the renewing of my mind had started to take its place.

All the old ways of thinking were slowly becoming undone.

Chapter Four – The Unbecoming

The statement you are about to read is something I had never been told, and it changed my life forever.

"Jesus gives His life to you, and through the authority of His Spirit in you, you can change and 'repent' from the way that you see things. This is what it means to be empowered by the Spirit of Christ!"

God knew that we had no power over sin and the lies of the enemy. I spent years of my life trying to put a fortress up against sin, only for those walls to come shattering down repeatedly. I have met hundreds of Christians who struggle with the internal war against their flesh. They continue to fail and identify with feelings of unworthiness, defeat, and weakness.

If you have ever struggled with sin, it doesn't mean that God will disown you. It means you are human. And just like every other human in the bible, you will face moments of trials and temptation. This is why God has given us the Holy Spirit.

Imagine this... God watched Adam and Eve who were created in His very own image fall into the deception of the serpent. He did not kill them. He did not throw them away. And even though their disobedience was not pleasing to

Him, He still considered them loved and worthy enough to send His only son to right the wrong that they had committed.

If we try and fight our battles in our own strength apart from God, we are too weak, and will lose every time. But if we align ourselves in perfect union with Him, we will find HIS STRENGTH in our weakness to be more than enough to overcome.

In Romans 8, the bible says, *God sent His own son in the likeness of sinful flesh and as an offering for sin, He condemned sin in the flesh.*

The Passion Translation says:

"Yet God sent us his Son in human form to identify with human weakness. Clothed with humanity, God's Son gave his body to be the sin-offering so that God could once and for all condemn the guilt and power of sin."
(Romans 8:3)

This is a powerful scripture. It tells us that Jesus came to the world as a man. He was fully God, wrapped in the form of man. The bible also tells us that Jesus was tempted at all points so that He would know what it felt like to be human. This means, there is no struggle, circumstance, or emotion that Christ has not endured. He took it all upon himself to know us, not to condemn us. He did not have to stand on street corners and protest to point out that people were living in sin. That is what the law was for. Instead, He came to show compassion and love people into the kingdom.

"Repentance was His message, but love is who He is."

(Ask yourself this question)

How many days of your life did you live perfect before Jesus made His home in you?

None right?

(Now ask yourself this)

Since Jesus has made His home in you, have you lived every day perfect?

The answer is no. Perfection is a human distinction, not a human attribute.

Only God is perfect, and Jesus was the only perfect human.

You see it is only with Jesus that we are made right with the Father, and it will forever be this way. For years of my life, I pictured Jesus the Son of God as the poster child of heaven. I felt it was my duty to be more like Him, and if I could not be like Jesus, God would want nothing to do with me. That is what religion taught me. I held this belief and even heard it backed up with scriptures like, "Be holy as I am holy." (Leviticus 19:2)

It made sense to me at the time. I figured that if my life had been such a wreck without God, that I was now supposed to make Him proud with my efforts and performance. I thought that if He was proud of me, that He would shower me with blessings and gifts. But I had to earn it.

This is the kind of thinking that sets the bar so high that I question – Do most Christians have the slightest understanding of the realness of Jesus in the flesh? I dare to say, most would not even recognize Him if He were standing in the room with them. Jesus was perfect and still is in every way. He doesn't expect us to be perfect. This is why we must have a union relationship with Him because it is only through Jesus that God sees us perfected and is pleased.

John 14:6 NKJV - "I am the way, the truth, and the life. No one comes to the Father except through Me."

If we could accomplish pleasing the Father on our own, then for what reason did Jesus have to come down to earth to die? Couldn't He just have appeared, said some words of encouragement, cheer us on a little, and tell us "See you later if you try hard enough?"

We somehow have overcomplicated the story and in return created a religious idol. We set standards of "our team vs.

your team," and if you cannot live up to the standard, you are not as holy as us, and you will not be accepted by our God. Intimidating rules and strict guidelines give off a "you better sit in the dark while you clean up your act" feeling to so many people which in turn does more damage than good.

I have talked to a great number of people during outreaches across America, and have heard so many times the response, "there is no way Jesus would want anything to do with a dirty backsliding sinner like me."

Have you ever heard someone you know say that?

It sounds a bit crazy! But we see it. In every denomination people are always categorizing themselves to their own standards of holiness. It removes grace and holds on to legalism. It pushes people away from the gospel.

I believe if the original followers of Jesus were alive on earth and could see the doctrine debates and religious confusion of today, they would publicly rebuke the church, reform to the text of love, and start over from the simple foundation of Christ's life and His grace for every one of us.

When we read in Romans, that Christ came to identify with our weakness – It should give us a new and refreshing understanding of how good God really is.

The first part of the sentence I think every Christian on earth will agree to. It says, *"God sent us His Son in human form..."*

It is the second part of the sentence that provokes religion.

It says, *"To identify with human weakness..."*

God sent His Son Jesus not only to take away the sins of the world but to identify with the weakness of human nature. This means Jesus identified with your flesh and carnal way of thinking. I know this statement seems like we are subtracting divinity from Jesus who is the holy Son of God, but to the contrary it is the opposite. When we as human beings, mix our own ideas and objectivity with His grace, this is what takes away from the sovereignty of Jesus.

> *"The addition to Jesus takes away. The subtraction of us adds Him."*

When we perceive the way things should be or what we think should happen, even if they are beautiful things, we automatically disqualify the life and will of Jesus in our journey. But if we yield all human perception and allow Jesus to be the voice in our daily lives, we will find there is a fine tuning of the heart when turned towards the direction of the Father.

This is an issue for most people. We have been taught since childhood that to be a success in this life we must work hard and labor, and we must live with a demand for the things of the world.

The bible tells us something completely different. It repeatedly gives examples of failure and defeat for not following the directions of the Lord. Throughout the entire text, every character's story shows the challenges of disobedience. The garden of Eden, the infidelity of King David, the stubbornness of Peter, and Paul's persecution of Christians are all examples of disobeying God.

There is only one story of obedience through and through. It is the story of Jesus. Jesus will forever be the only one who did not fall into temptation and sin. He was pure and blameless before God. He lived a holy life and was obedient to be the perfect sacrifice for us. Our only hope for salvation is that we detach ourselves from everything in this world and attach ourselves to Him.

We have a luxury as believers to release our old ways of worrying, thinking, and reacting. We have been given the Holy Spirit and mind of Christ to start trusting, believing, and responding based on what the word of God says.

I found freedom for the first time in my life when I realized that Jesus did not come to judge me by His expectations, but He came to receive me as imperfect as I was, and He took my judgement upon Himself. Even after salvation, I truly had not felt the release of the guilt and shame from my past until I accepted the grace of His love for me.

It had to register in my heart and get past the stronghold in my mind; that Jesus, the Son of God, came down from His throne to identify with me. He dove deep into my world to give me a brand-new life and took on the pain of my mistakes, my guilt, and my shame. He didn't deny me for who I wasn't. He accepted me for who I was. I finally understood His love for me. My whole life I had been under the impression that God wanted to judge me and that to please Him I needed to fulfill a list of approval rules.

It is deception and disobedience that keeps us from God. And what Jesus did, was bring us back to Him. All that anyone must do is see this truth, start believing it, and start living it.

Changes will begin to happen when you submit your life to Christ, and there is always much to learn about those changes. There is an unbecoming in our mind that must take place as a born-again believer. When our perception is renewed by God's word and His truths, we are empowered to know that Jesus is our hope in every circumstance.

It is by grace and by faith that you are saved! Nothing and no one can separate God's love for you. He placed the value of His Son's life on yours, so that you could be set free from the bondage of sin and darkness.

You have been made new!

2 Corinthians 5:17 NLT -This means that anyone who belongs to Christ has become a new person. The old life is gone; a new life has begun!

Chapter Five – The Grounded Theory

I hope that by now, some of the religious ways of thinking are breaking free from your mind. I have come to realize that so many people escape the bondage of sin and jump into the bondage of religion just as I did. I pray that this book is ministering to your heart, and that you start to take moments throughout your day to simply get away from the noise and meditate on God's word over your life.

Jesus said, *"if you have seen me then you have seen the Father"*. It is apparent many have received God's grace through Jesus but have never fully understood the power of His grace.

God is not challenged by your mistakes and failures. Through the cross we have been forgiven and justified. We are redeemed from the curse to live a life in perfect union with Him.

God knows that the enemy is a liar, and He knows that the enemy's attack on your life is to convince you of who you are not. The word convince is the root word of conviction. Therefore, if you are convicted, it is the gathering of thoughts in your mind, emotions, and motives to be convinced of something. Religion will tell you it means to be convinced of all the things you are doing wrong. But that is far from the truth.

God is a loving Father; He gives even the worst sinner the opportunity of salvation. He loves all His children, even the ones who disobey. He didn't send the Holy Spirit to follow you around and point out your sins. His purpose for conviction is to convince you of your newly created identity and the power of the finished work.

Grace turns human conviction to a desire to live a righteous life. I always tell people it is ok to want to make God proud, but do not lose yourself in trying to do so. He already loves you so much that He paid the highest price for you. You are already accepted.

The way we see ourselves as children of God, and the way we see God as the Father, plays a major role in the understanding of our relationship with Him.

There is an analogy that I refer to as 'The Grounded Theory.'

Being 'grounded' is a form of punishment used by parents to discipline their children. It refrains from physical discipline and instead focuses on punishment that removes positive reinforcement or other privileges. (For example: going out with friends, using the internet, playing video games, or watching television.)

As a child, I used to get "grounded" as punishment for misbehavior. It was normal to expect whenever I disobeyed or intentionally did not follow instructions. Many years later, as an adult, I started using this form of discipline in my own children's lives. I did not want to physically abuse them or cause any grief, so I used the 'grounded' method of punishment to influence accountability for their actions. I figured that it would persuade them to take responsibility and obey my commandments. I didn't realize the viewpoint that I was unknowingly introducing to them.

One day the Lord gave me a revelation. And because of what He showed me, I never grounded them again.

The action of grounding someone for their disobedience creates a perspective that can misinterpret how we see God as our Father. I have often heard that people view God through the same lens they see their earthly parents through. If this is true, it is easy to understand why some see God as a vengeful and wrath filled dictator, rather than the loving and caring Father that He really is. So many times, Christians have failed to represent His love and have created a misconception of who God is. Often this leads people to Atheism (rejection of God), or Misotheism (the hatred of God).

Did you know that the root of Atheism is unbelief? Think about that for a moment...

So, if the root of Atheism is unbelief, then what is a Christian who lives in doubt and unbelief?

The only difference is the words they speak. But in their hearts, they both are empty of trust and faith in God.

If a person believes that God is angry all the time and judging them, then they will never know how good He really is. And if they do not know His goodness, they will never know repentance.

Romans 2:4 NASB - Or do you think lightly of the riches of His kindness and restraint and patience, not knowing that the kindness of God leads you to repentance?

It is the grace and mercy of God that allows us to see Him rightly. Knowing His love for us and believing His love for us takes away our guilt and shame. The love of Jesus becomes a beautiful ray of light that pierces through the darkness and delivers a stone-cold heart to a softened place of healing and freedom.

It is the power of the Holy Spirit that has changed humanity for generations, and without the understanding of God's goodness, there is no liberty.

There is a story of a man named, Richard Wurmbrand. He was a Romanian pastor who was imprisoned for 14 years and tortured every single day. His beatings were severe, and the torment he endured was extreme. But because he knew the love and goodness of God, Richard held on to his faith and survived the gruesome events. After all the years of persecution, he was finally released from imprisonment. He continued his life preaching the gospel and telling the story about his suffering.

These are a few of His most famous and powerful quotes:

"God will judge us not according to how much we endured, but how much we could love."

"There were two kinds of Christians: those who sincerely believe in God and those who,

just as sincerely, believe that they believe. You can tell them apart by their actions in decisive moments."

"To believe in Him is not such a great thing. To become like Him is truly great."

- Richard Wurmbrand

Richard was a man of great faith. Through all the brutality he never gave up. This man held the hand of Jesus during his darkest hours in prison. And just like Paul the apostle, he considered it joy to suffer for Jesus.

Only a heart so in love could take such pain, and only a person madly in love would go to such great lengths. I pray that no one reading this book would ever be faced with such a challenge, but if one day you do, I pray that courage and the boldness to never give up overtakes you. And just like the story of Richard Wurmbrand, that because of your faithfulness to the Lord, millions of lives would be saved.

To know that we are loved and accepted by God not only removes the guilt, but it also empowers us to withstand the attacks and persecution of the enemy. If we hold on to guilt, it keeps us stuck with a growing fear of being alone, isolated, or abandoned.

For me, there were feelings of guilt and rejection that came from being grounded. In most cases, things that I enjoyed playing with as a child were taken away from me. I was told to go to my room and think about the thing I had done. Even though it was evident that it was my fault for being in trouble, I still felt anger and bitterness.

If it is true that we often see God through the same lens we see our natural parents, then it is not a surprise that those of us who have experienced the rejection and guilt of being grounded can feel like God has the same approach if we invertedly or intentionally fail Him.

But if God punishes those that fail Him, then I ask this question...

Why did Jesus go through punishment?

Before I had the revelation of God as a good and loving Father, I had the presumption that he was an angry judge. I always pictured the story of Adam and Eve, and how God must have been disappointed and angry with them for deliberately going against His commandment. But now looking at the story through the lens of His grace, we see that God was not mad at them at all. In fact, He chose to still show up for their meeting that day. He did not ground them or reject them. He didn't burn them up with His vengeful wrath. He came to show them love and concern. He presented Himself as a caring Father, but it was the guilt and shame of their actions that kept Adam and Eve from seeing His acceptance and great love for them.

Genesis 3:8 NASB - Now they heard the sound of the LORD God walking in the garden in the cool of the day, and the man and his wife hid themselves from the presence of the LORD God among the trees of the garden.

Based on scripture, there is no definitive proof that God would regularly walk with Adam in the garden, but the passage's implication seems clear. If the first time He chose to walk in the garden with Adam and Eve was the day they sinned against Him, it would have been conspicuously odd. When we read in the bible about God walking with people, it normally suggests closeness, intimacy, and fellowship. I would like to believe He had a personal relationship with them prior to their disobedience. The natural proposition is that God often did this daily "in the cool of the day," but the difference this time was that Adam and Eve were afraid because they had sinned.

So why did God kick them out of the garden?

It was not because He was angry with them and wanted to 'ground' them from their privileges. The truth of why He made them exit the garden is found in Genesis, chapter 3 - verse 22.

Genesis 3:22 GNT - Then the Lord God said, "Now these human beings have become like one of us and have knowledge of what is good and what is bad. They must not be allowed to take fruit from the tree that gives life, eat it, and live forever.

God knew that because of their disobedience, they had become separated from Him. He made the decision to save them, so He sent them away from the tree of life. If they had consumed the fruit from the tree of life, they would have entered an eternal separation from Him, and He did not want them to be permanently disconnected.

God was and He always will be love. He is not in the business of condemning His creation. He protects us and is devoted to convincing us of how loved we are. He sent Jesus to fix what was wronged from the beginning. And because Jesus was the perfect plan for the salvation of all God's children, we have been set free from the grip of darkness. Praise God!

This means - all the guilt, the shame, and accusations that try and hold us back no longer have a hold on us. The power of God's love crushes every lie of the enemy!

In scripture, Jesus calls the devil *'the accuser of the brethren'* (Revelation 12:10)

It is the devil's tactic to lure us into condemnation and spit out accusations of our sins. He is the annoying and recurring voice that continues to try and make us feel guilty for not living up to the expectations of our daily lives. His voice can be a consuming arsenal of de-functioning and controlling thoughts that plague our minds with abusive and traumatic titles based on our failures and imperfections. He is constantly at war against you to convince you that you are not accepted and loved. He wants you to feel that you can never be the person that God has created you to be. He points to faults, and he lures you away from God's truths.

God wants to pour His goodness into our present lives. It is at the price of His precious Son Jesus that we get to experience His righteousness. If we fall into the trap of believing the lies of the accuser, it is easy to disqualify ourselves from receiving it.

Most people do not understand the unconditional kind of love that God extends to us. If we assume that God is a vengeful and wrathful Father, this assumption leads us to believe that the moment we mess up, He takes away His happiness and love from us to teach us a lesson in failing Him. If this were true however, God would have to apologize to Jesus for making Him go through such horrific torture for man's disobedience. It would mean that the price of redemption didn't fully rest on the works of Jesus, but required more work that Jesus could not or did not do. That would mean it is up to the sinner to finish the task, even though fulfilling the task was something no one could ever do before.

That sounds conflicting, doesn't it?

If anyone believes there are extra efforts that we must do to be made right with God, it minimizes the life of Jesus and takes away from the power of the finished work. It would also make the Father a liar.

Here is the truth…

Jesus' sacrifice was the final sacrifice. God does not need an additional effort to be done to fulfill something that Jesus has already fully completed. Your only way in is to believe in the Son of God who paid an eternal and valuable price for you. Once you have received it, you live a life fully surrendered to the will of God, sharing this good news of His salvation for the world.

In my book the Beautiful Change I share this nugget of truth….

"When the veil was torn, God came for you. Heaven paid a high price so that you could return to Him as a son or as a daughter. There is no longer a separation from Him.

By exchanging your life for His, He washes your sins away. He changes you from the inside out. He mends your hurts and takes away the pain of the world. His love is complete, and it fills the void inside of you. His love is relentless, and it pursues you beyond all the chaos, the darkness, and the oppression.

I believe that when Jesus who was perfect in every way, hung on the cross, you were on His mind. And it was your life that He thought was of such worth to be paid for by His Holy Love!"

- *The Torn Veil, from The Beautiful Change*

For a good number of years in my Christian journey, I understood it was through faith in Jesus that I was forgiven and had received my salvation. But I believed that my life was under the radar, and the Holy Spirit was always following me around to make sure I didn't slip up. It was a never-ending battle of fear and burnout trying to stay on God's good side.

This is the definition of 'the grounded theory'.

If God still showed up in the Garden of Eden the day His creation disobeyed Him, then we must realize that He will never depart from us. He has a longing desire for His children to know His love for them. And if God wasn't walking around the garden that day and handing out punishment... then why would He choose today to start handing out punishment in your life?

This means that your mess ups, your disobedience, and your negligence are not reasons for God to 'ground' you.

Do you think that your sins are worse than the first sin of Adam and Eve?

The truth is Jesus took your punishment.

For your sins, He was beaten.

For your sickness, He was whipped.

For your disobedience, He was nailed to a cross.

And for your transgressions, He faced death.

This is the Beautiful Exchange given by Him.

Jesus rescued you from the eternal separation of God!

Hallelujah! He saved us all!

At no point will God ever send you to your room in anger. He doesn't shout at you for disobeying Him. He doesn't strip you of your worth or blessings. He doesn't hold your future in balance based on the fulfillment of a perfect life. He is not an angry parent with bitterness towards you because you failed Him or shamed Him publicly. He's not a God that wants to isolate you until you have decisively acknowledged the ramifications of your mistakes. He isn't a Father that grounds His children.

Although we must all face the outcomes to our choices in life, it is not the will of the Father to control us through fear, manipulation, or condemnation.

He is absolutely and endlessly in love with you.

And nothing you could ever do or not do can take away His unconditional love for you.

Chapter Six – God's Not Mad at You

I recently had some business cards printed for the purpose of sharing the gospel. After years of practice, I recognized the need for simple ice breakers to start up conversations. There seems to be a sensitivity when it comes to outreach and street ministry, and I believe it is due to tactless methods of using judgement, humiliation, and condemnation to try and preach people into the kingdom. For this reason, I thought it would be a good idea to have a card that starts a welcoming conversation about the love of Jesus. It's an easy way to share the good news of salvation.

The card reads, *"God is not mad at you. He's Mad about you!"*

This is the foundational truth of the gospel.

If we look back at the way God was perceived before Jesus came, we see that people feared Him, but it wasn't a reverential fear that was motivated by love. They had an actual fear of being destroyed by God's wrath. In chapter 20 of the book of Exodus, God wanted to directly speak to the Israelites, but they were afraid and sent Moses to be the mediator between God and themselves.

As we discussed before, God's wrath was once and for all poured out on Jesus for every one of us. Jesus cleansed us from all wrongdoing and made us right with God. Never at any point in the life of Jesus on earth did He condemn the unbeliever. He did however bring corrections to the pharisees who claimed to be followers of God. He rebuked the religious beliefs that God was angry at all people, and He gave us a new viewpoint of God's love for us and His grace.

There is something beautiful about God's grace. Grace doesn't give us the license to sin and get away with it, but it does allow us to make a choice without being persuaded by fear. God is a gentleman. He doesn't manipulate us into making the choice to follow Him. He had a plan from the moment He created the universe. He wasn't caught off guard when the devil chose to rebel against Him. He is and forever will be the victorious one in every situation.

I often say –

"God has never lost a battle and He is not going to start with losing yours."

Remember this – God already knows every situation.

The love of God is something way more definitive and exuberant than we could ever fathom. This means the greatest imagination cannot comprehend the magnitude of His love. Our humanistic definition of love often has boundaries and stipulations, but God's love is something so much bigger. It is not limited by human conditions.

Jesus, the son of God, made things right with the Father. He carried our burdens, and His sacrifice paid the price for us to have a brand-new life. Now through faith in Him, every person can receive and experience this new life that is full of His power and grace.

We must always remember that God's love is unconditional for His children.

It is not about our opinions. It is about His love for us.

It is not about our worldly successes. It is about His love for us.

It is not about our wrong doings or right doing. It is always about His love.

I am convinced that a big problem in most people's lives is the fact that they do not understand the freedom that is given by the love of God.

For two decades of my life, I made bad choices. Those choices left me with court cases and legal circumstances that required me to have monthly supervised check-ins and make financial payments to institutions. My bad choices had left me with a trail of responsibilities that would keep me unwarranted and out of any more trouble. I often notice this pattern in people who have lived the same kind of lifestyle that I once did. There is a sense of freedom that is removed due to the consequences of their actions.

In a legal court system if you do not step up and take the responsibility for your actions you will get into more trouble, and it leads to a warrant being placed for your arrest. (The definition of a warrant for your arrest is - to take the body of the person accused of an offense, to be dealt with according to law.)

All humanity was bound to the law of God. Truthfully, we each were destined to receive the punishment we deserved. Every man and woman would have been held accountable for their offenses made against God's law, but

Jesus took our place. He alone was the worthy lamb who was sacrificed for our offenses. He took the warrant for us and was crucified on a cross. He became the accused. His life took the legal action that we all deserved, and He delivered us from captivity by taking our punishment. This act was once and for all! It was the final judgement and atonement. Praise God!

Here is some good news! - There are no more warrants for your arrest for the guilty things you have done. You have acquitted!

This is what true freedom looks like.

No more warrant, no more punishment, no more questions, and no more records. God has delivered us by the redemptive blood of His Son. We are free!

The problem is most people don't have a renewed mind and the understanding that they are free. It sometimes seems they are stuck with the mindset that they deserve to be punished. Negativity rules their life. They live in the realm of negative feelings towards themselves and a continual cycle of feeling bad every moment they make a wrong choice, or yet even think about making a wrong choice.

In the Garden of Eden, they only knew of being created in God's image. It was the only way they had ever felt. They had never done anything outside of the mind of God, and they were fully clothed in God's righteousness. But when the devil in the form of the serpent questioned God's words over Adam and Eve, he became a co-creator in how they thought of themselves.

The devil cannot be the sole creator of anything without the assistance of our agreement in thinking and doing. When God gave man and woman the ability to create with His own personal power – the devil hijacked their thoughts and attacked their identity. He knew that he had no power over God, so he reached down into his dirty bag of tricks and pulled out the one trick that he knew would throw God's children into a world of confusion. He deceptively planted the seed of unbelief. (Read Genesis 3 - "Did God really say?")

The devil told the lie that God withheld information from them. That same attack of unbelief has not changed since the beginning. It still threatens the lives of God's children. It creates the question of being invaluable. But here is the good news! Satan is defeated. His lies are no longer a threat to us. They hold no weight against the truth of God's love and His word! Our identity is found in Jesus.

To understand God's goodness is to understand His truth, His love, and His faithfulness. His heart for humanity is beyond comprehension. Not even the angels and demons can grasp the infinite unconditional love that the Father extends to us. We are not constricted. We are not tied down to a one-sided view of who God is. He has given us free will. Our ability to make the choice is the thing that captivates all of Heaven. God is not sitting on His throne pointing His finger in judgement and forcing His children to accept Him. He has given us free choice to choose Him and to surrender our lives to His will.

In the Garden of Eden, Adam and Eve lost their inheritance by accepting unbelief rather than accepting the truth from the mouth of God. It was by their choice that they chose to disobey God. In the same way, 2000 years later, we are not forced to obey God or believe in Jesus.

"It is the song of the redeemed that shakes all of Heaven."

Imagine with me for a moment - a picture of heaven and all its glory.

Seated on the throne is the God of all creation and generations. He is God the father, God the Spirit, and God the son.

Power shines through His radiance from the magnitude of His perfection. Every angel surrounds His throne, and the heavenly hosts play their glorious instruments and sing. We read in the book of Revelation about the amazing and beautiful creatures that are around Him and lift the highest praise to exalt Him. I've always pictured white robes and white feathers, with streets made of gold, and all His creations on their knees bowed down and worshiping Him.

One day the Lord gave me this incredible vision…

I pictured heaven just like this. Hundreds and even thousands with hands lifted. Suddenly, out from behind the multitude… from the outer most part of Heaven, a small little voice was heard. It was faint and very distinct. Then I saw God shift the direction of His attention. The Lord stood up from His throne and all of heaven was silenced. Suddenly the small voice was amplified to a loud cry.

I could then hear this was a prayer of distress, someone saying "God please help me, I need you!"

I witnessed the power of that small prayer! The heavens began to rumble, and the ground began to shake. God with a furious love thundered in a loud and powerful voice!

He said, "Bring them to me!'

And Jesus His Son ran into the darkness to find that someone. As they returned, Jesus carrying a man, God proudly declared, "This man who cries out is my son in who I am well pleased!"

All of heaven shook in an uproar of praise!

There is power in the song of the redeemed! That in all of glory even the smallest heart cry can be heard. And there is something about this desperate cry for God's love that shakes the foundations of heaven.

This is the relentless, furious, and unwavering love of God!

The love that goes to great lengths to reach the lost, broken, and most unworthy of sinners!

We can't earn it. We don't deserve it. But He paid the highest price to restore you back to Him.

God is not mad at you.

Chapter Seven – Determination Over Defeat

There is a story of a young man who followed a successful guru. The young man one day told the guru that it was his desire to become a successful leader like him. The guru took the young man to the ocean and directed him to walk out into the water. The man stopped when the water had reached his waist and looked back at the guru.

The guru said, "keep going!"

The young man walked further until the water was around his neck. He turned to the guru.

"Keep going!", the guru shouted.

So now the man walks head under the water and stayed under the water until he could no longer hold his breath. He rushed out gasping for air, looking to seek the approval of the guru standing on the beach sand.

The guru walked out into the water to meet the young man, and with smile across his face said, "Until you want to be successful as much as you want to breathe, you will never see the results you are dreaming for."

The story tells us about a young man who had a desire to become successful. The older and wiser guru gave the man an example to understand that what he desired would come at the price of determination.

I remember when I first came out of addiction. My whole life had been flipped upside down. I had to disconnect myself from people and things. I had to make a choice. I could continue in the darkness I was living in, or I could choose life... the life of Jesus. For me it wasn't a program or a preacher that changed my life. It was the power of God that in my final moment came in like a gasp of air. I had exhausted everything else in my life. It was the final straw... I didn't have anything else except God. It was in desperation that I cried out for Him. And for the first time in my life, I felt like He chose to be in the room with me personally. In that moment, He wrapped His arms around me.

I started seeing miracles and the manifestations of His Spirit shortly after. I didn't want to waste another moment. I knew I was created to share the love of Jesus. I didn't need a stage or pulpit. I would pray for people anywhere and everywhere. There was an empowering feeling of God working through me that kept me from looking back at my dark past. It was the goodness of God and the realization that He had given me hundreds of opportunities to choose Him that made me burn with passion. He was the only one that had never tuned His back on me. It became my desire to live for Him.

Since the moment I fully surrendered my life to Jesus, I have tangibly encountered His presence thousands of times, and witnessed immeasurable experiences of the Holy Spirit. The testimonies I share aren't to boast about myself. They are to tell others about God and to show His love and realness.

I've witnessed jaw dropping miracles and I have seen multitudes of people receive salvation. I've witnessed firsthand the power of God move again and again...

Take hold of this truth -

In all these wonders, I have learned that all the prophetic words, all the teachings, all the prayers, all the songs, all the stages, all the miracles, and all the callings of our lives are From Him - Through Him - and For Him! It's all His.

The bible tells us that faith is pleasing to the Father, and it is by faith that we live our lives as Christians here on earth. The key implementation to faith is trust. Trust is everything.

Our obedience and willingness to trust God is what makes us different from the world. As a believer our lives should shine with assurance, trust, faith, integrity, grace, and power. This is what the first century church walked in, and it changed history.

Jesus told us in John 16:33 - *These things I have spoken to you so that in Me you may have peace. In the world you will have tribulation but take courage; I have overcome the world."*

What seems to be the challenge of the believer is trusting our Father, believing that we are His, and having faith that He is in control. In most case scenarios, we must decide if we will follow our instincts, experiences, and emotions... or will we follow the word of God and trust that His word is the final word over our lives.

I am completely and madly in love with Jesus. My heart beats to encounter Him and to worship Him every day of my life. If He did not love me, I would not be here to write this book.

But... just because I chose to follow God, this does not mean that I haven't failed or made a mistake since the day I was saved. This is the beauty of His grace!

When my mind was engulfed by darkness, I never even thought about the sin I was committing. After I surrendered my life to Jesus to walk in righteousness, the thought of sin plus the awareness of trying not to sin plagued my mind. It created what I call 'sin consciousness.'

It took me many years to understand that 'sin consciousness' ruled my life. Sin consciousness is the awareness of sin. To make it simple, it is the focus and awareness of all sin in general.

It takes away your focus from all the things that are right. You can also say, it takes away from seeing all the things Jesus did for your life.

I often use the analogy of wet paint on the wall. If you walk into a room and there is a neon-colored sign hanging up that says, "do not touch, wet paint". I guarantee at some point, someone in the room will touch the wall... Just to see if the paint is still wet. And guess what? I can guarantee that person will come back again later to touch the wall to see if it is still wet.

Now imagine if you walked into a room and there was no warning sign hanging up. You wouldn't even think about touching the wall. Why would you?

This is the power of sin consciousness over one's life. It makes you look at the distinction between good and evil.

Do you see the connection of eating from the tree of knowledge of good and evil? It is the tree in the garden of Eden that separated humanity from living in the fulness of trust in God. It created a knowledge of self, rather than freely living in His image, knowing all things were created by Him and through Him. Deception, disobedience, and sin created a false doctrine that we as God's creation needed to do something outside of His love for us to survive.

I had never realized the power of sin consciousness in my life until I understood this.

Carefully examine the beginning and what we read in Genesis. The attack against humanity was that there was something that God was holding back from Adam and Eve. The devil in the form of the serpent proposed the idea that there was something more that could be done to be accepted by God.

That is Religion!

I can't tell you the number of people I have encountered that have told me they didn't feel loved by God and in their shame didn't think they were worthy enough to be loved by Him.

I had to realize how much God loved me to find freedom from guilt and shame. And I pray you will come to that realization as well to find freedom in your own life!

Before I move on in this book, I am going to pray for you right now -

"Jesus, you are everything. There is no one like You. When the world stops spinning and Your presence comes in, you break the lies of the world. Nothing else matters when your presence comes. Just to be with You is worth more than life itself. For all those reading this book right now, I pray all lies over their life, all guilt, all shame, and all condemnation be broken off them today! In the name of Jesus!"

Sin consciousness had created a perspective in me that had kept me bound in my walk with Christ. The devil has been attacking lives for an exceptionally long time. I am not giving him credit but stating facts when I say he is good at what he does. If it were not for the Holy Spirit all humanity would be powerless.

In scripture, we read - *No wonder, for even Satan disguises himself as an angel of light. - 2 Corinthians 11:14 NASB*

Satan is a dirty, lying, and deceiving, snake. What makes him so dangerous to humanity is his cunningness to appear not only in the darkness... he also presents himself in the form of a counterfeit light. Without discernment we can often fall into his sneaky attacks and by trying to contend with the enemy in our own strength we end up burned out and exhausted.

After 33 years of trying to do things my way I knew what it was like to feel burned out. I finally broke and surrendered everything to Jesus. I had exhausted everything in my life. I burned bridges and hurt people. I was alone and felt completely abandoned.

"In my weakness I cried out, and in His power, He answered me."

After coming to know Jesus as my savior, I started out on this journey to be the best man I could become. I went to church, prayed for people, gave money, and read my Bible every day. This is what I was taught Christianity looked like. I attached myself to other people who knew scriptures and said they loved God. I was invited to study groups and cook outs. My children were accepted in Sunday school and began to enjoy it. I was watching God do miracles in all the needs of my life. It was a beautiful and new beginning.

After some short time, I began to feel like there was more to my walk and I wanted to go deeper in the knowledge of God in my life.

It seemed now though, that by trying to go deeper in knowledge, I started to notice faults in other people. I started to notice things that didn't line up with the scriptures. I witnessed gifted men and women who had been in ministry for years do things they knew were completely against God. I didn't have the capacity to fully understand grace and this created a religious perception of everything that I was seeing. I began to feel judgment in my heart towards others. I was deceived by the enemy to think that I was somehow better than everyone else because I had left a life of sin to follow God. It was not until I was humbled to see how much God loves every one of us, that those chains of religious bondage were broken.

The intent was that I wanted to become a better Godly person. The deception was that I let the things around me distort my view of God's grace and became aware of what I was seeing rather than the truth of God's word.

It is important to surrender to the Lord, and that we are always in His perfect will and plan. But it is equally important that we have the determination to keep going and never give up. Even if what you see does not align with what you know.

Jesus never asked us to follow people. He said, "Follow Me".

There is a story about a woman that went to her Pastor and said, "Pastor, I won't be going to your church anymore."

The Pastor responded "But why? "

The lady said, "I saw a woman gossiping about another member; a man that is a hypocrite; the worship team living wrong; people looking at their phone during service; among so many other things wrong in your church."

The Pastor replied, "Ok, but before you go, do me a favor: take a full glass of water and walk around the church three times without spilling a drop on the ground. Afterwards, leave the church if you still desire to do so."

The lady thought: This is going to be too easy!

She walked three times around the church as the Pastor had asked. When she finished, she told the Pastor she was ready to leave.

The Pastor said, "Before you leave, let me ask you something else. When you were walking around the church, did you see anyone gossiping?"

The lady replied "No."

"Did you see any hypocrites? "

The lady said "No."

"Anyone looking at their phone? "

"No."

"You know why? "

"No."

"You were focused on the glass, to make sure you didn't stumble and spill any water. It's the same with our life. When we keep our eyes on Jesus, we don't have time to see the mistakes of others. We will reach out a helping hand to them and concentrate on our own walk with the Lord."

The moral of this story is in the pastor's response to the lady of his congregation. We often allow things to take our focus off Jesus which leads us to a place of a defeat. If we keep our focus on Jesus through our day-to-day experiences, we will find that the word of God is true, and He is faithful to keep us. If we don't allow what we see to take away from the relationship we have with Him, we can detour from a path of devastation and defeat. It is the knowledge of God's faithfulness that rises our faith to the surface. It becomes a 'God conscious.'

Hosea 4:6 says, *My people are destroyed for lack of knowledge; because you have rejected knowledge, I reject you from being a priest to me.*

The deception of the enemy in our lives is to make our problems bigger than God.

That's a lie. There is no problem bigger than God.

The reason so many people struggle with their faith in the Lord is because they have never experienced the power of God in their lives. At the first sign of trouble, it is easy to run back to the things that feel most comfortable to us, and sometimes even give in to defeat.

You must always keep your heart in the truth. No matter how tough it gets and no matter what the attack is on your life, you must always keep your focus on the prize. You must always do what you know to be right. Never let the lies of the enemy steal your joy.

People choose things in life - like careers, real estate, and money. They go after these things no matter what gets in their way. They wake up early and go to sleep late. They work endlessly and collaborate with gurus and life coaches. They are determined, and they don't stop until they achieve what they are striving for.

If the world can be overtaken with such determination for things that are not eternal. Shouldn't we as believers be more determined for the eternal glory of our loving Father?

Defeat is not an experience that God wanted us to have. Humanity was already defeated before Jesus came. But because of the cross and the power of the blood, all victory now belongs to Him. Now He has chosen to share that same victory if we never give up!

Vince Lombardi, a famous American football coach who won 5 NFL championships once said, "Winners never quit, and quitters never win."

In your own personal walk of faith… you choose to follow determination or defeat.

"Your story will either be OUTCOME or OVERCOME!"

Chapter Eight – Passion Over Performance

If you want to know what Grace looks like - look at Jesus. Jesus is truth and He is grace. The definition of grace is favor unbalanced on our behalf. This means God is not currently fighting for you. He has already fought for you, and He won! We as His believers stepped over the finish line the day that we chose to follow Him. By accepting Christ into our hearts, we have made a home for Him. His Spirit now dwells in us.

For centuries, men and women were bound by the law of the old covenant works and they were given strict rules to obey, but none could accomplish obeying every law. Therefore, Jesus came and fulfilled the law in our place. This removed all works on our behalf and allowed us to be made right with God on His behalf. This is good news!

Even 2000 years later, we are still free from the curse of sin and death. Grace has crushed the lies of the deceiver. Truth has been written in the hearts of all those who are willing to simply believe it and receive it!

There came a point in my life when I got tired of feeling depressed and not good enough. I was tired of having worn out and bad days. At the end of myself, I finally surrendered to God. He filled me with His Spirit and empowered me to stop living in a place of defeat, and to start living from a place of victory! From that moment, I never had to believe another lie or accusation against my self-worth again.

This included the realization that there was nothing I needed to do to impress God, except to obey and have faith in His Son. It was a game changer for me!

I suddenly recognized the power of the cross. And after so many years of believing in God, I was able to see I had yet to surrender the part of me that identified to performance.

Picture this...

A sinful man goes to a Sunday morning church service. The preacher is long winded but delivers a powerful message of salvation.

The preacher extends the invitation to receive the life of Jesus.

He says things like...

"His death was your death."

"His burial was your burial."

"You are now a new creation."

During the end of service prayer, the sinful man walks down to the front of the church and prays the prayer.

Later that night, the born-again believer walks home. Alone and full of good cheer, he stops at the local gas station for a stale hotdog and a cold soda. He continues home, but along the way he encounters old friends. In the newness of his decision to be a Christian, he fails to interject the conversations with what had just happened at church. Feeling a little ashamed, he continues his walk home.

Upon his arrival, he hears his sick mother crying for help. He comes into her bedroom to change her sheets and night gown – all the while, wondering where this Jesus that he just received is…?

He takes a shower and heads to bed with so many questions left unanswered. His main question being… "if God is real? Why hasn't he changed anything?"

After a few short months struggling financialy and facing old habits, he decides that trying to carry the load of being good and following Jesus is way too much for him to handle.

He feels he has enough problems of his own and now he is trying to carry the weight to do the right thing. He asks himself, "What's the point?", and so he turns back to his old sinful ways.

Does this sound familiar? If not your familiarity, do you know someone who has felt this way?

This is the lack of knowledge!

You see, so many times in the church we have failed to explain the covenant made by Jesus to His Father which is the basis of our salvation. The negligence of the church has left many people filled up with dreams of blessings and prophetic words. Innocent people have been handed promises for salvation rather than promises of the savior… I'm going to say that again.

"Innocent people have been handed promises FOR salvation rather than promises OF the savior."

Our default is weakness. In this world there has been nothing offered that is eternal except the gospel. So many people waste their lives worrying about their status and stressing things out of their control. Day after day, humanity is plagued and beaten down by attacks against our identity. Even the greatest Christians can fall into the sinister traps of the enemy.

Without the Holy Spirit we do not have authority. Without the Holy Spirit we do not have discernment. Without the Holy Spirit we do not stand a chance. But with the Holy Spirit, all things are possible! We are not broken. We are not torn down and destroyed! We are not lost! We are not left alone! We are not headed down a dead-end road!

Our mind should stay fixated in God's words. The Truth about who we are is determined by who He says we are.

2 Corinthians 4:8-9 NKJV - We are hard-pressed on every side, yet not crushed; we are perplexed, but not in despair; persecuted, but not forsaken; struck down, but not destroyed

We must focus on our new life in Christ. Can you imagine what Paul the apostle had to go through? He spent years in dark prisons, far worse than any prison today. He went through days and maybe even weeks of torture. He was beaten and starved. Even in those dark places, he never gave up and he never denied Jesus. He was so in love with Christ, that he preached the gospel to the ones who tortured him.

In western culture, we celebrate scriptures like Philippians 4:19 that *says, "I can do all things through Christ who strengthens me."*

Yet, I wonder if people truly know what it looked like when Paul wrote these scriptures.

Around 61 or 62 AD the letter to the church of Philippi (the book of Philippians) was written by Paul while most likely being imprisoned in Rome. The Roman prison was dark and hideous, rank with the stenches of feces, and the guards cared very little for their prisoners.

Picture Paul chained to a wall, hungry, beaten, and probably without a change of clothes for months. This is the picture of what I see every time I read Philippians 4:19. We often fail to realize the persecution and violence Paul was under.

Paul was persecuted for his message of grace. It was the immense power of God in that message that kept him going.

The Bible says, the thief comes to steal, kill, and destroy. You will often hear preachers define the thief in this story as the devil. It can be true in some cases, but if Jesus came to give us power over the devil and the enemy is already defeated, then does the thief occasionally slip out of his imprisonment to torment us when God is not looking?

No! The devil has been defeated once and for all. He is an animal locked up in a cage. He has a loud roar and no bite!

In Revelation, Jesus calls Satan the accuser. This means he cannot touch you; he can only accuse you. A little old lady once told me that after many years she finally realized the devil is a toothless snake. "He can try to impart fear, but he has no fangs."

The accuser reminds you of your past. He cannot see into the future, and he can't control what happens in your future. His only offensive attack against you from now until eternity will be to try and convince you that you are not loved by God. That's it. It is his only attack. He is the deceiver. The deceiver highlights your fault and steers you away from your freedom.

We give the devil too much power over us. God says he has been defeated. The only power he has is when you agree to give him the authoritative right over mind, will, and emotions. It was the same in the garden of Eden, he obtained power by deceiving Adam and Eve.

Religion teaches us performance because performance will get your mind to a safe place. The devil initialized performance right there in the garden. His attempt to destroy humanity was the simple suggestion that God did not impart His whole self into them, yet if they would choose to do something out of their own free will, God the creator would be pleased to make them just as magnificent as He. Oh, what deception! They were already created in His very own image. They had no knowledge of sin or darkness. Their perfect world was not to be in search of something bigger and better. Their perfect world was having no distractions of God's goodness or the recognition of sin. The fullness of life was simply knowing Him.

Religion is eating of the fruit of knowledge and placing efforts on how to obtain God's favor. Religion teaches us how to die. You may have even attended a church service where you were told that you need to learn to die daily to obtain holiness, yet if this were true what was the point of Jesus' performance over your performance?

Apparently with that way of believing, your performance is the foundation of your salvation, and the sacrifice of the Son of God was just a highlighter to get you to notice your failures in life.

People don't need to have a finger pointed at them to understand they are living in sin. Let me rephrase that, some people might need to feel condemned to come to the realization of their need for salvation, but most people have a pretty good understanding of right and wrong based on moral values.

The idea of dying daily can become the awareness of trying not sin – which in turn leads to 'sin consciousness.' Dying daily is in the scriptures, but what Paul was referring to was sacrificing His freedom to be imprisoned, charged, and persecuted daily. Paul wasn't a man living in the present age saying I need to wake up tomorrow and do better because I have been slacking on my morning devotionals.

If it is true, that the death of Jesus was our death, and the burial of Jesus was our burial... then it also true that the resurrection of Jesus was our resurrection!

Dead people don't need to die again. Dead people need life. Jesus teaches us how to Live!

We have been recreated and made flawless in the eyes of God, and we have been given the gift of a righteous life through Jesus.

Hebrews 10:10 NLT - For God's will was for us to be made holy by the sacrifice of the body of Jesus Christ, once for all time.

You cannot add on to what Jesus already did...

Hebrews 10:16-18 NKJV - "This is the covenant that I will make with them after those days, says the Lord: I will put My laws into their hearts, and in their minds, I will write them," then He adds, "Their sins and their lawless deeds I will remember no more." Now where there is remission of these, there is no longer an offering for sin.

The protection, blessing and well-being of the old covenant was based on behavior. God's people under the old covenant worked for forgiveness and the atonement of their sins. After the new covenant made between Jesus and the Father, God's people freely received forgiveness and a final atonement through the impartation of Jesus' righteousness.

This is the truth of our salvation, and truth is not a subject or a doctrine... He's a person. His name is Jesus.

It is the passion of the Christ that has saved us. It is His love for us that escapes us from sin and hell. He alone is the one found worthy of cleansing us of all unrighteousness and restoring what was once lost in the beginning. His grace and mercy for us far surpasses any works or rule to gain the acceptance of the Father.

I am confident that the precious life of Jesus is valued so much by God, that when He sees you, He overlooks your failures and sees the mutilated blood bathed body of His innocent Son. This is the power of passion over performance.

John 3:16 ESV - For God so loved the world, that he gave his only Son, that whoever believes in him should not perish but have eternal life.

Romans 5:8 ESV - But God shows his love for us in that while we were still sinners, Christ died for us.

1 John 4:10 ESV - In this is love, not that we have loved God but that he loved us and sent his Son to be the propitiation for our sins.

2 Corinthians 5:21 - For our sake he made him to be sin who knew no sin, so that in him we might become the righteousness of God.

Chapter Nine – Stillness Over Stubbornness

Psalm 46:10 AMP - Be still and know (recognize, understand) that I am God. I will be exalted among the nations! I will be exalted in the earth.

In the previous chapters, I explained the necessity of determination and passion. Now I want to talk about stillness.

I once heard it said, "the challenge of a true believer is knowing when to get out of the boat or when we are supposed sit still in the boat."

In our walk of faith, we must be keen to the Spirit of God that leads us. We must desire the will of the Father and learn to act when He prompts us. Jesus said His sheep hear His voice and follow Him. But it is also equally important that we understand the moments in our relationship with Him when He is asking us to be still.

Discerning the voice of the Holy Spirit will always lead us in the right direction. I have encountered many crossroads in my journey of faith. I've had to cut ties and walk away from some people. Other times I've had to leave places that I wanted to stay. It wasn't necessarily because they were bad or dangerous. It was because I had to learn that where

I was going and where God was taking me was somewhere different.

You may be asking –

"If the Holy Spirit is in you, why should you have to cut ties or walk away from any situation?"

"If we are filled with the Holy Spirit, then shouldn't we be a light to everyone around us?"

Yes, I agree that we must always be a light in the dark places of the world, but I acknowledge that we must sometimes get away from the distractions and the noise to hear the voice of God. Even Jesus went away from the crowds to be with His father.

If Jesus had to cut ties to remain in the perfect will of the Father what makes us any different?

Deep down in my heart, I burn with a fiery ambition to see the lost saved for the kingdom of Heaven. Yet along my journey I have had to learn that not everyone in my life is there to lift me up and bring me closer to my destiny in Christ.

Yes, I do believe in the power of the Holy Spirit. I do believe in discernment. But I also know that not everyone can swim across waves that you have been called to.

"I've had a lot of friends come and go. When I was shaken, it also shook them. And when I had to cross the floods through the storms, none of them could swim. Sometimes, God takes us places that the people around us can't follow. Even in the midst of our struggles His plan is complete.

Whatever storms that you are dealing with, and if you feel alone, remember that it's only you that can conquer the waves!"

God is in the business of completion. As a matter of fact, He has already completed your situation and even more so, completed the situation of the world we live in. All things are in His hands and all things are finished by His Grace.

We live by the finished work of the cross. It is the root of our belief and the foundation of our lives as believers. The life of Jesus was given for us so that we may have an eternal and divine life here on earth and get to experience a life with Him now.

The act of believing occurs simultaneously with trusting, and trusting is how we grow in faith. Faith is the key to unlocking peace, joy, and happiness.

The renewed mind of someone who has been born-again is developed by reading God's word and proclaiming it over your life. To exercise our faith, we must believe what we say we are believing in.

Paul says it this way –

"Our faith in Jesus transfers God's righteousness to us and He now declares us flawless in His eyes. This means we can now enjoy true and lasting peace with God, all because of what our Lord Jesus, the Anointed One, has done for us. Our faith guarantees us permanent access into this marvelous kindness that has given us a perfect relationship with God. What incredible joy bursts forth within us as we keep on celebrating our hope of experiencing God's glory!" (Romans 5:1-2 TPT)

This is a powerful statement in Romans 5, and I believe there is a monumental breakthrough here for those who have lived with feelings of guilt, shame, and condemnation. Most Christians have faith that God will do something for them. But the truth is - He has already done everything we need Him to do according to His finished work.

Verse 1 of this Chapter tells us, it is our faith in Jesus that transfers God's full righteousness to us. This means - there is nothing more for us to do than to believe and have faith in Christ. Your old life has been exchanged for a heavenly grace filled life. Nothing you can do or can't do will keep you from God now that His Son paid your debt in full to be restored back to the Father.

The only disconnect is not receiving all that God has offered you by simply rejecting and refusing to believe this free gifted freedom.

It's a challenge for most people to tear down the walls of their guarded hearts and realize that there is no need to live in fear, pain, regret, or rejection. Once we surrender our will and emotions, we can then take on the life of

Christ, which is a life of the finished work - full of His power and grace!

If our salvation truly depends on the finished work of the cross alone, then we must also see that we lack nothing beyond this gift of the Son of God.

Jesus is everything. He is the promised land. He is the prize.

Ages ago God's people were desperate. Longing and crying out they prayed for the day the Messiah would come down and rescue them. That day finally came the moment Jesus was born in this earth. He was the chosen one. He was the anointed one and the savior of the world. The moment He fulfilled His purpose on earth, He gave up His Spirit, so that the same Spirit that raised Him from the dead would be poured out on His people. Praise God that the enemy has been defeated once and for all!

John 1:29 NASB - "Behold, the Lamb of God who takes away the sin of the world!

As a believer and born-again creation full of the Spirit of God, your life will never be the same. Confidently I say this – your life can now and eternally be filled with peace and joy.

Scripture tells us – it is no longer I who live but Christ who lives in me. This means your old life is dead and gone, buried six feet under. You die with Christ, and you are raised with Christ. All the work necessary to be received by Him has been completed. You now stand victorious with the life of Jesus and in His finished work you can be still and know.

Now look at the second part of the sentence in verse 1 of Romans 5…

It says, *"He now declares us flawless in His eyes!"*

You might not see yourself flawless, but God does!

You might not see yourself healed, but God does!

You might not see yourself as an overcomer, but God does!

You might not see yourself loved, but God does!

You have been set free and made new by the precious blood of the Jesus! Hallelujah!

I know there are matters in life that we face, and that there are real problems in existence that get the best of us at times. I'm not excluding the fact that these situations happen, but I am saying there is hope for every circumstance.

God tells us to bring all things before Him and not be anxious for anything. I agree wholeheartedly. If oppression, fear, and anxiety are challenges in your life… yes, bring it to the Lord and lay it down at His feet. Start praying from a place of victory! Begin to praise Him for removing these burdens and rejoice that the enemy has been defeated! Thank the Lord for all His goodness and declare with your mouth that the work has been finished!

You have been given the fortune of liberty to be still, and enjoy a life taken care of by the Father.

It was the realization of God's grace in my life that reformed my way of praying. I stopped begging Him to do something about my problems and I started thanking Him for His finished work. That is when something amazing happened! I learned to sit still in my prayer closet. It became a place of rest. I stopped praying to God answers. I understood that I no longer needed to worry about anything. I put my trust in Him, having faith that He knew the circumstances I was facing. The only thing I wanted - was to know Him more… and it was then that I started to see miracles!

I continue to find myself strengthened and refreshed in difficult times by simply agreeing with what Jesus has already done. When I sit still in reverence and thankfulness for the finished work, my heart becomes full of the enjoyment of His presence. When I am with Him there is not a care in the world that can convince me of how bad life can be.

Being still in His presence removes all the distractions that can lead to doubt and fear. Truthfully, it's hard to find yourself worrying about anything when you turn the affections of your heart to Him.

There is a worship song that says, "When you walk into the room everything changes." This is true. When we invite Jesus into our lives, everything changes. He wants us to understand how much He loves us and offers Himself so that we put our complete trust in Him.

Life itself is consistent of emotions and relationships. People are not motivated by rules and religion. They are motivated by feelings, and God's love conquers all. When we pull away and get alone with Him, there is no corporate worship, no corporate prayer, and no corporate acknowledgement. It is just you and Him.

Just like John on the island of Patmos in the book of Revelation, Jesus gives revelation to His loved ones. Legalists in religion will say it is blasphemous and impossible that the God of the universe would speak to impudent, small, and unworthy sinners. They will argue that God is only makes Himself available for the righteous, and that He is selective by only choosing who He finds worthy. I used to think this way too.

For years I felt there was a level of God's standard that could only be reached by continual sacrifice of myself every day. I thought the life of a believer was supposed to be a test. No fun was allowed, no personal desires, and no messing up was on the long list of rules that I considered to be God's holy expectation. I pictured myself under the radar, and for every moment that I made a bad choice, I needed double the amount of time to prove my worth by beating myself up. Just like in the old covenant – I carried the burden of wanting to do something in my own power for the atonement of my sins.

I didn't understand the love God had for me, and that He wanted a relationship with me, or even more, that He wanted to speak to me.

Ask yourself these questions.

What would a relationship with someone be like if there was no communication? How much more important is it that there be communication between man and his Creator?

God wants to speak to us through the Holy Spirit. He speaks to our soul, and His truths enlighten the spirit man inside of us to align with His perfect will. He is always working on our behalf. I say 'He is always working' but I don't mean He is always putting His hands to the plow. He has already finished the work of His promise through Jesus.

What I mean is, He has already conquered the strategic battles of our lives, and the victory is now manifested by us simply believing. He reminds us that we are loved, and He fills us with His assurance. He draws us to Himself, and He speaks to us the goodness of who He is.

God is not contemplating your life and the possibilities of the outcome for your current situation. He isn't sitting on His throne in Heaven worried about what the outcome may be. He is always in control, and His abilities are at work in us through every moment of every day. This is the greatest gift and promise. The fulfillment of His grace is available to all who believe. It has no favorites, it has no method, it has no requests, and it has no struggles.

When we rest in the finished work of the cross and come into agreement with the life of Jesus, our faith activates the outcome.

His grace gives us a reason to be thankful and assured.

We have been given a life worth living and nothing worth regretting.

Stop worrying and start praising!

It is imperative that you learn to live in a place of stillness and let go of stubbornness.

You have nothing to lose and everything to gain!

Chapter Ten – What You Fall in Love With

"What you are in love with, what seizes your imagination, will affect everything.

It will decide what will get you out of bed in the morning, what you will do with your evening, how you spend your weekends, what you read, whom you know, what breaks your heart, and what amazes you with joy and gratitude."

"Fall in love, stay in love, and it will decide everything."

- from the book, *Addicted to Busy, by Brady Boyd*

I have had the privilege of leading outreaches and sharing the gospel in hundreds of cities, and I've noticed that many people "believe" in God – yet very few have a personal relationship with Him. A true relationship with God requires a willingness to put aside any selfish desires that would keep us from becoming His disciple. Sometimes the hold of this world on our heart is impossible to break. The call to be a Christian requires a genuine faith in the sufficiency of Christ accompanied by radical change in practice.

In our union with Jesus, we become motivated by love and not by demanded rules. He gave up His life for me, and because of His grace, I now willingly choose to surrender my whole life to Him.

To be alive in Christ means to be fully dead to yourself. It means that you are dead to your way of thinking… and dead to your way of doing. It means fully surrendering your life over to His will, so that you can be born again and made a new creation. We must let go of the things of this world and set our thoughts to what God desires, even if it means giving up anything and everything.

I understand this is a tough revelation to swallow, because in the natural realm people struggle to work themselves approved and to be accepted in areas of their lives where they feel they need to become a success. Long hours, sleepless nights, and years of hard work are fought through to reach the goals that we set for ourselves. And once those goals are achieved, it isn't easy to think about letting them go. We often can come up with a way that seems right to follow Christ based on our life experiences, even if we know in our hearts that God longs for us to go deeper. The world will always choose selfish ambition over selfless obedience.

Aren't you glad that Jesus was not selfish?

He certainly didn't give His life as a sacrifice for fame and fortune, and it surely was not for a position to uplift His self-esteem.

The Gospel is a love story about a King who sacrificed everything for His bride!

You are His bride, and He is your King!

He came for the one He loves. He came because He knew you needed to be rescued.

You have seized His affection, and His love for you is beyond anything you could ever dream of. He gave His life for you, and because of His sacrifice you have been brought into union with Him eternally.

He fell in love, He stays in love, and His love for you is everlasting!

Ask yourself this question:

What have you fallen in love with?... Because that is what will possess your heart.

Chapter Eleven – Weakness

**Be sober, be vigilant; because your adversary
the devil walks about like a roaring lion,
seeking whom he may devour.
- 1 Peter 5:8 NKJV**

Notice in 1 Peter 5:8, the scripture says the devil is "like a lion", it doesn't say "he is a lion."

It also says he seeks 'whom he may' devour. This means he must have permission. That permission comes by the agreement we make with our mouth, our heart, and our actions.

The devil has no authority over a person empowered by the Holy Spirit, but he will use anything he can to make you fall into fear. He will test you in places that he knows you are the weakest. His best attempt is to make life's circumstances become so unbearable that we would finally give up and lay down like a wounded gazelle waiting to be devoured.

The enemy lies and deceives to make you feel insecure and defenseless. He will use anything and everything to discourage you. He wants to convince you that there is no hope for your problems. He wants whatever situation you go through to lead you further away from God, and further away from the truth of God's Grace.

Paul says - We are destroying sophisticated arguments and every exalted and proud thing that sets itself up against the [true] knowledge of God, and we are taking every thought and purpose captive to the obedience of Christ. (2 Corinthians 10:5 AMP)

Along my journey, I have had moments where my faith was weak. I needed to be reminded of God's love for me, and to redirect my focus back to the truth of who God created me to be. No matter how indecisive and distraught my mind became, I had to take ownership of my thoughts and believe God's word over my life.

It is the duty of the mature believer to take every thought captive. We must not let the lies of the enemy extinguish the love and knowledge we have of Christ. When we feel offended and emotionally hurt, our focus shifts from Jesus to ourselves. But if we truly are dead to our old self and have been given a new life in Christ, then we've relinquished the right to live by our feelings. I'm not denying the fact that emotions are real, and circumstances can sometimes be challenging, but let me remind you that we serve the one who has overcome the world.

In John 16:33 Jesus says, *"here on earth you will have many trials and sorrows. But take heart because I have overcome the world."*

When fear and doubt gain access into the heart, devastation sets in, and the old man who is supposed to be buried starts to resurrect. By reacting to our emotions, it is easy to make wrong decisions and irrational mistakes. It is imperative that we know the truth of God's word, so that we never lose sight of who we are. The enemy knows if he can get to us when we are in our weakest moments that we are more susceptible to his schemes. However, it is in our weakness where the grace of Jesus Christ perfects our strength.

When you submit to God and resist the devil, you are empowered by the Holy Spirit to overthrow the oppositional forces against you!

But He said to me "My grace is sufficient for you, for my power is made perfect in weakness." Therefore I will boast all the more gladly of my weaknesses, so that the power of Christ may rest upon me. For the sake of Christ, then, I am content with weaknesses, insults, hardships, persecutions, and calamities. For when I am weak, then I am strong.
- 2 Corinthians 12:9-10 ESV

Paul encountered grace on the road to Damascus. Even though he had made a career out of persistently destroying God's people, Jesus forgave him. In 2 Corinthians, God's words to Paul are an encouragement that the power of grace is a continual sufficiency that will strengthen him against any "weakness" that may come as he presses on.

How we perceive our past and the things we've experienced can disable or enable us in our journey. We must choose whether we will live in regret, or will we look to God's grace that empowers us to persevere? Just like Paul, we have all made mistakes and bad choices. It can be haunting and oppressive for some, and for others it enables them to see God's grace. It becomes the fuel to their fire that gives them the power to be free.

"Our perspective of the way something is will create the way our heart interprets the situation."

My walk of faith has not always been easy. The story of my life is full of ups and downs. On the outside, when you look at me, you might see an author, an evangelist, a pastor, a husband, a father, or a friend. What you don't see are the moments I have spent on my knees praying to God. There are years of trials, struggles, battles, wins, defeats, faith, pain, joy, tears, laughter, and crushing... but through it all a REAL RELATIONSHIP with my creator!

I often say, "If the world could see not just the scars and tattoos that I have on my body, but the scars that are on the inside, then just maybe they would have a flash or a glimpse of just how much Jesus has forgiven them."

After all I've been through and rescued from - I will never sell my life short, and I will never put a price tag on the Life of Christ. Because of Him and only Him my life has been redeemed!

"It's not a Religion. It's a Relationship"

There will be days of uncertainty, but it is God's love that sustains us. Grace isn't released to us by our good deeds. It is released to us through the mercy of Jesus. It is His affection towards His people and His bride. God knew we would all face failure and make wrong choices.

He also knew we would one day be alive right here and now. He knew you would be reading the words on the pages of this book.

Whether you choose to accept these words or not, it's your choice.
Whether you choose to accept defeat or not, it's your choice.
And whether you choose to accept His grace for you or not... That too is your choice.

Jesus died for you. He has forgiven you, and He has given you the gift of grace if you choose to receive it.

"Christianity is not supposed to be hard to stay saved."

Receiving our salvation is the easiest thing we can do. It doesn't require us to work. We don't have to physically be crucified, buried, and resurrected. Jesus already did that. All we must do is receive what Jesus did by believing and having faith in Him.

People in times of suffering and weakness turn to God for help. And rightly so, for He is the savior of the world, and only through Him can we be rescued and redeemed. Yet sooner or later in their walk, people often grow weary. The spark of their born-again experience burns out, and they lose the enjoyment of their salvation.

Whether it is a noticeable change or if it is small gradual changes, eventually trust in the sufficiency of God's grace is hindered by doubt and lack of confidence. This makes it difficult to keep the faith and clouds the vision to see Gods strength in our circumstances.

Be strong and courageous, do not be afraid or tremble in dread before them, for it is the Lord your God who goes with you. He will not fail you or abandon you.
- Deuteronomy 31:6 AMP

The devil launches attacks against our mind, will, and emotions. Guilt and regret anchor themselves and then become poison to the soul. The truth of the word of God is the antidote to the internal thoughts against our identity in Christ. Without hearing the word of God, it is impossible to comprehend His grace. When the storms of life come crashing down, it is a default behavior for people to be filled with fear, doubt, and unbelief.

The Bible says, "Faith comes by hearing and hearing by the word of God. (See Romans 10)

Hearing His word and believing His word deflects the attempt of the enemy that is at work to diminish our faith.

In the wilderness, Jesus responded to the devil's temptation by saying, "Man shall not live by bread alone, but by every word that proceeds from the mouth of God." (Read Matthew 4)

It is a matter of life and death to have faith in God's word. It is crucial that we as believers read the bible and choose to believe what it says!

God's truth is the only response we need... especially in our times of weakness. Having an immovable faith releases His grace and power into our problems. Just like when David stood before Goliath and called him an uncircumcised philistine.

David wasn't just insulting the giant by calling him names. Circumcision played a significant role in the conditions of the old covenant agreement between God and man. David was declaring that Israel and its people had a covenant with God. He knew that God was on his side as he stood against the philistine army, so he didn't cower down in fear. By faith he stood his ground, and he marched forward with confidence to take down the giant that stood in his way! (Read the full story in 1 Samuel 17)

This is why we must live by the word of God.

When the enemy comes at you with a challenge, be like David!

Take a stand, speak to that giant, and declare your victory by faith!

Pause for a moment and ask yourself – "What is God saying about me right now?"

"Right Believing produces Right Living."

Believing the word of God over your life means that you are coming into the agreement of His love for you. It is acknowledging the sufficiency of His grace for you. When you believe right, you will automatically produce the fruit of right living without even trying.

When the accuser comes to pull you down with guilt from your past, the Holy Spirit reminds you of who you are. This is the power of grace over your weaknesses.

Grace helps you to remember what God has said about you. It empowers you to walk out what He has called you to. You no longer are destined to live in shame and the regret of your past because the blood of Jesus makes all things new! The burdens of yesterday may have lasted through the night, but today is a new day!

Grace has overcome guilt!

Weeping may last through the night, but joy comes with the morning.
- Psalms 30:5 NLT

Chapter Twelve – Grace Over Guilt

I want to share with you again the paragraph God put in my heart when I first came up with the title of this book,

"People have a problem with themselves. They exclude their own type and feel who they want to be is unobtainable... They believe the lies that they are ugly, weak, worthless, useless – and live in guilt and shame. Only Jesus can see through the mess to bring to light who you really are. His blood washes away the labels and lies over us. And His love speaks a better word.

That is His grace!
It empowers you to become who you really are!"

After years of looking for answers and striving to walk out righteousness as a Christian, I struggled with the discouraging feeling of never being good enough. I had yet to understand His grace and union in my life, and so there was a false sense of separation that weighed on my ability to do right by focusing on everything I did wrong. I carried a lot of grief and strife from the performance of behavior modification. I was worn-out by religion, with feelings of guilt and condemnation that I believed were keeping me from receiving the blessings and fulfillment of God's perfect will for me.

Then one day, while I was reading in Colossians, the Holy Spirit opened my eyes to see something that changed my life forever...

Colossians 1:26-27 TPT - There is a divine mystery—a secret surprise that has been concealed from the world for generations, but now it's being revealed, unfolded and manifested for every holy believer to experience. Living within you is the Christ who floods you with the expectation of glory! This mystery of Christ, embedded within us, becomes a heavenly treasure chest of hope filled with the riches of glory for his people, and God wants everyone to know it!"

I suddenly realized that God's plan since the beginning, was that one day we would know His grace and to be filled with the fullness of His Holy Spirit!

What magnitude of love this is! That the creator of the universe and everything in it would come down and make His home inside of us. This awakening to the power of grace changed me forever. I didn't do anything good to earn it, and there is nothing possible I could have done to deserve it. God chooses to love us with all our failures and imperfections, even while we are still sinners.

This is the secret that the whole world and all of Heaven had been waiting for.

Up until now, it had been hidden… It was the mystery of every generation.

Paul says – "it is now being revealed to every believer to experience."

It is described as a heavenly treasure chest filled with the riches of Glory, and in other bible translations it says, "Christ in you is the hope of all glory."

Think back to those whose stories we have read in the Bible, for instance - Abraham, Moses, David, and even Solomon (the wisest man who ever lived). They had a passionate desire for the mystery of God to be revealed. They desperately prayed to be filled with the eternal power of the Holy Spirit. They all had moments of experiencing moves of God, yet none ever experienced the fullness of His Spirit manifested inside of them. It was impossible…

until Christ Himself gave His life!

Romans 8:11 NLT -The Spirit of God, who raised Jesus from the dead, lives in you. And just as God raised Christ Jesus from the dead, he will give life to your mortal bodies by this same Spirit living within you.

I often hear Christians say, that one day they will ask the persons of the bible - "What was it like to see the power of God?"

But I truly believe that when we stand in heaven, those we read about in scriptures will be so overtaken and amazed by the grace that God has given to us, that they will be the ones asking the question - "What was it like to be alive with the power and Spirit of God living inside of you?"

Ephesians 2:7-8 TPT - Throughout the coming ages we will be the visible display of the infinite riches of his grace and kindness, which was showered upon us in Jesus Christ. For by grace you have been saved by faith. Nothing you did could ever earn this salvation, for it was the love gift from God that brought us to Christ!

Our perspective must change from guilt to grace! We must understand how much God truly loves us and how much of a price He paid for us to be redeemed. His grace is everything, and it is the only thing that gives us hope.

Jesus is grace!

He is the hope of all glory!

Romans 5:1-2 TPT – "Our faith in Jesus transfers God's righteousness to us and he now declares us flawless in his eyes. This means we can now enjoy true and lasting peace with God, all because of what our Lord Jesus, the Anointed One, has done for us. Our faith guarantees us permanent access into this marvelous kindness that has given us a perfect relationship with God. What incredible joy bursts forth within us as we keep on celebrating our hope of experiencing God's glory!"

It is our faith in Jesus that gives us the favorable circumstance of being grafted into the family of the Father. We share in this marvelous kindness that has given us a perfect relationship with God, and we get to experience all His Glory!

Romans 8:17 says," And *since we are his true children, we qualify to share all his treasures, for indeed, we are heirs of God himself. And since we are joined to Christ, we also inherit all that he is and all that he has. We will experience being co-glorified with him provided that we accept his sufferings as our own." (The Passion Translation)*

We are God's true children! We have been qualified solely on the perfect sacrifice of Jesus to share His inheritance and all His treasures. Ephesians 2 tells us, that throughout the coming ages and in all of eternity we are the visible display of the infinite riches of His grace.

In the story of Adam and Eve, Adam felt guilt and shame, so He hid in the bushes from God. We read in scripture that God showed up in the cool of the day looking for Adam, but it wasn't to punish Him. God gave him the opportunity to repent, but instead, Adam blamed Eve for his sin and never took responsibility for his disobedience.

Shame and Guilt will always lead us into hiding. Just like Adam, when we mess up or have the feeling of failure, we tend to run in the opposite direction from the cross. It is the opposite direction of grace, and it's almost as if we run to hide in the bushes hoping that God will not see us and our imperfections.

God sees all things. He knows the intentions of your heart and he knows your thoughts. He chooses to love us, and He chooses to forgive. Your life is valued by the sacrifice of His only son! That is how much He cares about you! He is ready and willing to forgive anyone who has a truly repentant heart. All we must do is come to an agreement with His grace, and we will be set free from every act of sin and disobedience.

It really is that simple.

For years, my understanding of salvation was God coming into my messed-up life to change the world around me. It sounded good, but I found this was far from the truth. Although God does want us to welcome Him into our lives, the fact is, Jesus paid the price for our salvation so that we could come into the righteousness of His life. He fills us with His Spirit so that we are empowered to rise out of the bushes and walk back to Him.

What good would it be for God and Adam to both be standing in the bushes?

God is calling to each of us to come out from hiding and to be separate from the world. It's easy to be caught up in the idea of letting God into our mess, but He wants to bring us out of the mess and into His kingdom! This is where new life begins!

His kingdom is so much better than any world we could ever try and formulate for ourselves. As I said before, Christianity is not supposed to be hard to stay saved. It is simply running into the arms of a forgiving father and staying close to His heart.

There have been moments in my past where I have failed, and because of my mistakes I lived in regret and guilt. Even as a born-again Christian, the memories of my errors haunted me. It took me many years of prayer and council to chisel away at the feelings of self-inflicted pain. There were times that the guilt would burn so deep that it began to determine the decisions I would make in my life, and it left me feeling completely hopeless. It birthed an unhealthy fear inside of me that made me question if God would ever forgive me again.

When a person is broken to the extent of feeling they cannot recover from a mistake or something they have done, they are immediately greeted by the lies of the enemy that rob them from their identity in Christ. And if they feel they cannot recover from something that has happened to them, they will be immediately introduced to the fear of being hurt again. This cycle is a devastating blow to physical, mental, and spiritual health. It often leads to sickness, depression, anxiety, and uncontrollable addictions.

After years of struggling with guilt about my past, I finally concluded that I couldn't change the things that I had done. I also couldn't change the things that had been done to me. So, if the past wasn't going to change and the memories weren't going to go away, the only thing I could do was accept it.

Let me explain…

"Our perspective has to change from guilt and regret to acceptance."

While I was in bible college and working in the ministry, I made one of the biggest mistakes of my life. I was already saved, but I chose to step outside of God's will to go after something that was never meant for me. I gave in to temptation and in that moment, I allowed the spirit of lust to become my master. I purposely walked away from people and places that God had put in my life. I cheated, I lied, and I did everything I could to try and cover it up.

This was a repetitive cycle my entire life before I became a Christian, and here I was once again falling back into the same cycle of destruction that God had rescued me from.

Instead of facing my problems head on and speaking to the giant that stood in my way, I turned around and ran in the opposite direction. This caused me and the people around me immeasurable amounts of pain. I was broken. I felt lost. It was all my fault.

I was dishonest and I tried masking all the guilt and shame by blaming everyone else like Adam, but that didn't work. The weight of the condemnation became unbearable. I was exhausted, and I could no longer live with the lies. I finally came clean and repented of everything I had been hiding… but still the pain wasn't going away. I had fallen into the trap of the enemy.

Daily I was forced to face the question that has plagued humanity since the garden of Eden – "Did God really say?"

I'm sharing this with you because I want you to understand that even as a Christian, we can fall into the traps of the devil. We can still be persuaded and tempted. It is certainly still possible for believers to fall short of glory if we are not sober-minded and vigilant as the word tells us to be.

During my restoration, part of the process included investigating my past experiences from childhood to adulthood. I was faced with challenges of confronting fears and hurts from my past. I had to look at the details of my afflictions and come to the unbearable conclusion that I was still holding on to some things. It was painful to dig up the past, and it was even more painful to make the changes necessary for my freedom. I had to fully let go, and in the end after I surrendered it to God, I realized one thing.

I was still alive, and I was still breathing to continue my journey.

Through all the mess, Jesus had never left me, and He never abandoned me. He was always there, and He was always willing to forgive me. He was calling me higher, to rise from the bushes, and to come into His world. He loved me then, He loves me now, and He wants a relationship with me.

Honestly, I can't tell you why He would want someone like me, especially after all the things I've done in my life. There seems to be only one fitting conclusion… His Grace!

The end to this cycle of my life came when I made the decision to accept my past rather than run from it. I had to recognize that no matter how badly it hurt me and no matter what I had been through – it was all for the purpose that I would grow stronger.

There was a reason I had to walk through the fire and feel the pressure. There was a purpose in the pain and all those struggles. If I had not been through those trials, I would not have been challenged to find real freedom.

The acceptance of my past strengthened me. I stopped looking at the memories and feeling sorry for myself. I stopped using the excuse that I wasn't good enough and that I would never be forgiven.

My perspective changed, my heart changed, and my mind was renewed, so that once again I could feel the peace and presence of the Holy Spirit.

Throughout history God has never changed. In my circumstance, He still didn't change.

He has never lost a battle, and He's not going to start losing in whatever you may be going through in your life! He holds the victory!

The acceptance of my past allowed me to breathe again. It allowed me to grow. It allowed me to see areas of my life that needed to change. So, I repented my mistakes and surrendered my life fully. I wanted freedom from guilt, and I needed God's grace. I took ownership of my disobedience and I asked for forgiveness from those that I had hurt. I also learned to forgive everyone who had ever hurt me… but as equally important, I learned that I needed to forgive myself.

My whole life's perception had shifted. It was in my weakness where I found His loving arms once again. I didn't see the guilt, pain, and suffering anymore… I saw grace, growth, and strength - and along with His healing came a renewed measure of His unlimited power!

"Healing comes when we take a look at the role we play in our own suffering."

People are good at having reasons and excuses for how they react to life's circumstances. It is easy to put the blame on your mistakes and past traumatic experiences when you haven't let go of them. We collect detailed information about the way we have been hurt and the ones that chose to hurt us, and the list is long of memories that keep us stuck from moving forward. Some of you reading this book right now may be in the middle of an emotional and spiritual fight against your freedom.

I want to pray for you – "Father, I think you right now that your blood was the final atonement and the final word. Your love for us is immeasurable. Your grace for us is everything. I pray for the person reading this book, that you God will consume their minds and hearts with a holy fire to burn down every lie and stronghold of the enemy against their well-being. I pray for freedom of their heart, soul, and mind. I pray for the enlightenment of their being to come into full adoration of the Father, and that they may be renewed in their strength and identity. Teach them daily oh Lord that they are loved, they are forgiven, and they a redeemed by the blood. I pray for continual revelation of the gospel. Show them who they are in You and who You are in them. Thank you, Jesus, for your precious life given to us. We give all honor and praise to you. You are the only one and true savior. Amen!"

This gospel unveils a continual revelation of God's righteousness—a perfect righteousness given to us when we believe. And it moves us from receiving life through faith, to the power of living by faith. This is what the Scripture means when it says: We are right with God through life-giving faith! - Romans 1:17 TPT

Paul says the gospel is a continual revelation of God's righteousness. He says it is perfect righteousness given to us when we believe. This means the righteousness of God isn't a trophy we have earned by our works or good conduct. It is given to us by simply believing in Christ. You become righteous in God's eyes by receiving what His Son (Jesus) did for you.

Being filled with His Holy Spirit, you can live in peace knowing that God is pleased with you. Understanding this truth, empowers us to walk out righteuosness with God as a son or daughter. You will never be alone again and can live in freedom by having this faith.

For since we are permanently grafted into him to experience a death like his, then we are permanently grafted into him to experience a resurrection like his and the new life that it imparts. Could it be any clearer that our former identity is now and forever deprived of its power? For we were co-crucified with him to dismantle the stronghold of sin within us, so that we would not continue to live one moment longer submitted to sin's power.
- Romans 6:5-6 TPT

We read in Romans 6 that we have been co-crucified with Jesus.

By His grace we do not have to be physically crucified to a cross for our sins.

And by faith in Him, the stronghold of sin within us is dismantled.

This means sin no longer has power over us!

The sacrifice of Jesus fully submerged us into the grace of God. His love for us gives us the ability to choose life over death. We are no longer helpless to resist the devil. We now have the authority and power of the Holy Spirit.

You are not obligated to sin! Praise God!

When you are faced with the temptation to sin, or maybe the accuser is bringing up feelings of regret and shame, it is important that you learn to use those lies against you as fuel to your fire.

"Let the old life circumstances become a springboard into your NEW LIFE!"

The enemy will use anything he can to separate you from the truth of who you are.

He is not afraid of a believer that is physically dead, or one who is alive yet spiritually numb to the power they possess.

He is absolutely and utterly terrified of a believer who knows who they are in Christ and what Christ has done for them.

Any time you are faced with challenges, use it as a springboard to leap over the lies of who you are not, and stand upright with God's assurance knowing who you are. This springboard of truth allows you to resist the devil and by the loving grace of God walk out the identity of your new life as a new creation.

Your current situation may not be pretty. You may be dealing with unbearable memories. You may still have scars and trauma that you are praying through and being counseled through, but don't lose heart. God sees the mess and He loves making the mess clean again. His grace covers you when you are weak. It pierces through the depths of your worst pains and lonely nights. It brings to light the power of God's immeasurable goodness. And He wants you to receive it!

"Let your past become the evidence of the price that Jesus paid on the cross."

God is and forever will be.

He is the beginning and the end, and He is all that is in between.

He is the creator, and He is Lord over everything.

Yet, it was not until the sacrifice of His only begotten son, that He would be known eternally as the Savior of the world!

The redemption of humanity by the blood of Jesus on the cross was the way God chose to introduce salvation to His creation. It was and is the only way into His kingdom!

Another part to the acceptance of your past is realizing that your redemption from guilt to grace is the evidence of the value of Christ's life sacrificed. The life of Jesus is the most precious and valuable gift. It was a high cost for Heaven to pay the day that Jesus gave himself for us. By acknowledging your past as the evidence of the life of Jesus, you take on a new role as an adopted son or daughter. You can then put on the life of Christ by understanding that He did it all for you! He took on all the guilt, the shame, and the condemnation, and He destroyed the sting of it all, so that you would not have to live with it. And as you continue your journey of faith, He continues to pour out His life and Spirit into you!

Galatians 2:20 TPT - My old identity has been co-crucified with Christ and no longer lives. And now the essence of this new life is no longer mine, for the Anointed One lives his life through me—we live in union as one! My new life is empowered by the faith of the Son of God who loves me so much that he gave himself for me, dispensing his life into mine!

The new life of the believer is now empowered by Jesus the Son of God. He loves you so much that He gave His life for you. He knew that we needed Him. He knew that we couldn't face the enemy alone. He knew that we needed to be filled with His power. This is the importance of a real relationship with Him. Through His Spirit and His word, He has dispensed His life into ours!

Paul addressed the church of Galatia and reminded them that it was a gift to receive the Spirit of Christ. It wasn't by their efforts that they received.

What has happened to you foolish Galatians? Who has put you under an evil spell? Did God not open your eyes to see the meaning of Jesus' crucifixion? Was he not revealed to you as the crucified one? So answer me this: Did the Holy Spirit come to you as a reward for keeping Jewish laws? No, you received him as a gift because you believed in the Messiah. Your new life began when the Holy Spirit gave you a new birth. Why then would you so foolishly turn from living in the Spirit by trying to finish by your own works? Have you endured so many trials and persecutions for nothing? Let me ask you again: What does

the lavish supply of the Holy Spirit in your life and the miracles of God's tremendous power have to do with you keeping religious laws? The Holy Spirit is poured out upon us through the revelation and power of faith!
- Galatians 3:1-5 TPT

It is not by works that we have received grace. It is only by faith in the finished work that we have received our new birth. It is important that we now learn to live by the Spirit instead of turning back to try and live by our own efforts. If living by our own efforts didn't work before Christ, then surely living by our own efforts will not work after Christ.

Have you ever been thirsty?

Imagine a day where you've been outside working in the summer heat. Let's say you were parched and in dire need of some water.

If I came to you with a bottle of water, you wouldn't question me where that bottle of water came from. You wouldn't ask me how long I've had it. You wouldn't ask me which company made it or how much it cost. None of those things would matter.

You would open the bottle and drink your fill.

In the same way many people are suffering from a thirst for truth and righteousness, and in their efforts to find hope they go to church or reach out for help. Often, they can get good counsel by attending a church service or meeting with a minister, and in those moments, they are filled.

But what happens when they run out and there's no more to drink from?

Those who find a small glimpse of hope for their parched lives often feel the need to work at doing more to achieve more and satisfy their thirst. For example, pray more, tithe more, memorize more scriptures, or even spend more time at the church serving the ministry.

Though these are all great things to do, they do not satisfy the thirst. They can help alleviate the cravings, but it is only real intimacy with God that allows us to be fully satisfied.

My job as minister of the Gospel is not to show you how to put in work. It is to point to the work that has already been done for you. It is to disciple you and help you renew your way of thinking.

The gospel is the fulfillment of all things needed in our lives. It does no good for me to give you a drink of water and wish you good luck on finding your next drink. It is so much better that I not only give you the drink, but also point you to the living well that never runs dry!

That is the message of the gospel! There is one from which you can drink and never go thirsty again! His name is Jesus!

Discipleship is an essential part of the Great Commission.

The enemy's attack on your life doesn't stop.

When we lack discipleship, we don't know how to pray and fight through our battles. Most people have never been taught about the grace and power of God. I have had countless conversations with men and women that feel they are too far gone for Jesus to want anything to do with them. They have been hiding in the bushes for so long, they feel like God has abandoned them. This is a lie from the devil!

We all have different seasons of our lives. And in those seasons, we each possess the ability to make decisions based on our experiences or based on God's truth. If your life is like mine, it has been full of ups and downs. There have been moments where I felt the pure enjoyment of life itself, but there were also days I felt nothing at all. Those were days when I felt like I couldn't hear God and I was clueless about the things going on in my spiritual journey.

"In every season, find Jesus and never let Him go."

We must be certain that no matter what comes against us, and no matter what it looks like around us, we never take our eyes off Jesus. Just like Peter stepping out of the boat and into the waves – the moment he took his focus off Jesus he started to sink. (Read Matthew 14:22-33)

In every season you walk through as a believer, Jesus is with you.

Find Him.

Get into the word of God and find out what He says about your circumstances. Get on your knees and pray for His revelation to come. Sit still in His presence and allow Him to fill you with His goodness.

Don't fall into the traps of fear and deception. Put on truth and allow the gift of righteousness to lead you in every moment.

Renew your mind into His mind.

Take the thoughts against you captive and make the declaration that you are no longer the person you used to be.

Thank God for His Son and thank Him for the cross.

Tell your problem that you will not submit to the lies and tell yourself that you are a child of God.

You are forgiven and redeemed. You are blessed and not cursed. God is for you not against you. You are His, and He wants the very best for you.

His Son paid the full sacrifice for you to walk full in grace and never live in doubt again!

Deception is a liar, and guilt has no hold over you!

for whoever has entered God's rest has also rested from his works as God did from his. Let us therefore strive to enter that rest, so that no one may fall by the same sort of disobedience. For the word of God is living

and active, sharper than any two-edged sword, piercing to the division of soul and of spirit, of joints and of marrow, and discerning the thoughts and intentions of the heart.
- Hebrews 4:10-12 ESV

There is a wonderful working power in the renewing of the mind.

Allowing our perspective to change from guilt to grace and allowing the word of God to change the regret into acceptance heals the soul. His words speak truth over you, and it cuts through the lies. It separates the weight of the world in your life from the kingdom you truly belong to. By using the word of God and believing it over your life, you are given the discernment to make the advancements needed in your daily walk. It becomes a supply for your needs, and it is the reminder of how much you are taken care of and loved by Him.

So it is impossible for God to lie for we know that his promise and his vow will never change! And now we have run into his heart to hide ourselves in his faithfulness. This is where we find his strength and comfort, for he empowers us to seize what has already been established ahead of time—an unshakable hope! We have this certain hope like a strong,

unbreakable anchor holding our souls to God himself. Our anchor of hope is fastened to the mercy seat in the heavenly realm beyond the sacred threshold, and where Jesus, our forerunner, has gone in before us. He is now and forever our royal Priest like Melchizedek.
- Hebrews 6:18-20 TPT

In this passage of Hebrews 6, Paul ensures us of our strength and hope found in the finished work of Christ. In your journey from guilt to grace, you must always remember that Jesus is your hope. In every situation you face, He is the answer.

It is impossible for God to lie. So, if He vowed to create a covenant through His Son, then that covenant is sufficient. That covenant is grace! His decision and promise will never change.

When we run into His heart, He is faithful. He fills us with His strength and comforts us. We partake of an unbreakable hope for our lives. We become empowered to take the victories as spoils of war! We can seize everything that has already been paid for on the cross!

Our souls are held tightly by His grace for us, and this hope is what allows us to walk rightly just like Jesus did.

Our anchor is unshakably fastened to the mercy seat in Heaven!

Notice in the passage it says, Jesus is our forerunner.

In the footnotes of the Passion Translation, it refers to Jesus as the "trailblazer."

- *(6:20 Or "trailblazer." Jesus has blazed a trail for us to enter into the sacred chamber and seize the hope that has been fulfilled in his eyes already, to have a company of king-priests who will dwell with him in the holiest of holies and minister from there out to the nations of the earth. The clear implication of v.19-20 is that he takes us in to share his throne and his ministry as the royal Priest.)*

Because of what Jesus has done for you and me, we now share in God's glory with Him!

Remember Romans 5?

Through Him we also have access by faith into this [remarkable state of] grace in which we [firmly and safely and securely] stand. Let us rejoice in our hope and the confident assurance of [experiencing and enjoying] the glory of [our great] God [the manifestation of His excellence and power].
- Romans 5:2 AMP

We can now rejoice in this hope, and we can have a confident assurance that we get to experience and enjoy the glory of God. A life with Christ is a free life! We are liberated from guilt and shame!

There is no longer a dark cloud.

There are no more secrets and lies hidden in the closet.

We are now filled with His Spirit. And where the Spirit of the lord is there is freedom!

When you have this true freedom, you can forgive those who have hurt you, and most importantly forgive yourself. Forgiveness doesn't always look like restoration, but that's ok. It's not about the result of restoration. It is about letting go of holding on.

Unforgiveness lives in a heart that has been hurt and refuses to let anyone be happy, including the one who chooses not to forgive. It suffocates you.

I once heard a man say - "Unforgiveness is like drinking poison and expecting someone else to die."

When you let go of guilt and deception, it removes the mastery of something or someone over your life. It disconnects you from lies. It breaks the shackles that hold you back from healing and becoming the person that God created you to be.

Truth separates you from unbelief and the Holy Spirit empowers you to live a life full of grace!

In closing, I want to look at Paul the apostle.

Paul was one of the most influential leaders of the early Christian church. He played a major role in spreading the gospel during the first century. After his conversion, he evangelized all throughout the Roman empire. He started more than a dozen churches.

Paul is arguably considered to have written 13 books of the Bible - more than any other biblical writer. In Christianity, he is one of the most influential people in history. His epistles have impacted the world more than any other person besides Jesus.

But before he was known for all this, Paul was known for persecuting Christians. The Book of Acts tells us that Paul was even present at the death of the first Christian martyr - where he "approved the stoning of Stephen" (Read Acts 8:1).

Before becoming a follower of Christ, Paul was a prime example of a "righteous" Jew. He came from a God-fearing family. He was a Pharisee like his father, and he was educated by respectable rabbis. His Jewish credentials included his heritage, discipline, and zeal.

As a Pharisee, Paul saw Christians (who were predominantly Jewish at the time) as a threat against Judaism. From Paul's perspective, these people were blaspheming about God and leading his people astray. He believed that Jesus was a mere man and was therefore rightfully executed for claiming to be God.

And since Jesus' followers kept spreading the idea that Jesus was God, Paul thought Christians were the worst sinners to ever exist.

It shouldn't come as a surprise that Paul made his debut in the Bible as an intense persecutor of Christians.

When Stephen was stoned to death for preaching the gospel, "the witnesses laid their coats at the feet of a young man named Saul. . . And Saul approved of their killing him" (Read Acts 7:58–8:1).

(To clear any confusion - Saul is a Hebrew name and Paul is the Greek version of the same name. Similar to how "James" is the Greek form of "Jacob," and since most of the New Testament was written in Greek it makes sense that we see the Greek version of his name most after his conversion.)

Later, Paul asked the high priest for permission to take Christians (known as followers of "the Way") as prisoners:

"Meanwhile, Paul was still breathing out murderous threats against the Lord's disciples. He went to the high priest and asked him for letters to the synagogues in Damascus, so that if he found any there who belonged to the Way, whether men or women, he might take them as prisoners to Jerusalem." - Acts 9:1–2

On Paul's way to round up some Christians as prisoners, Jesus stopped him dead in his tracks and crippled him with blindness. (Read Acts 9:1-9)

Paul now knew the true identity and power of the one he had been persecuting, but he had yet to learn Jesus' grace and power to heal. And for that, he would need to meet more followers of Christ.

Paul spent the next few days with the very Christians he had come to capture, and he immediately began preaching the gospel of Jesus Christ. It caused mass confusion to Christians and Jews. It would take time for Paul's reputation as a Christian preacher to outgrow his reputation as a persecutor of Christians.

In his own accounts of his conversion, Paul says that Jesus appeared to him. (1 Corinthians 15:7–8)

He claimed that Jesus revealed the gospel to him. (Galatians 1:11–16).

His encounter on the road to Damascus completely redefined who Paul was, and it changed the purpose of his journey from silencing Christians to speaking out in support of them. Instead of taking away from their number, he added to it. And once Jesus redirected him, Paul continued this trajectory for the rest of his life.

Paul's notoriety as a persecutor of Christians made believers uncomfortable around him even after his baptism, and it took a while for them to believe that he'd really changed.

Paul's identity used to be rooted in being a Jew under the law, but after his radical conversion on the road to Damascus his identity as a Jew became secondary to his identity as a follower of Christ. He spent much of his ministry dismantling the idea that in order to be accepted by God, you must first fulfill the law. He crushed the idea of works to be saved and he emphasized the grace of God over guilt and condemnation.

He wrote powerful messages like -

Our faith in Jesus transfers God's righteousness to us and he now declares us flawless in his eyes. This means we can now enjoy true and lasting peace with God, all because of what our Lord Jesus, the Anointed One, has done for us. Our faith guarantees us permanent access into this marvelous kindness that has given us a perfect relationship with God. What incredible joy bursts forth within us as we keep on celebrating our hope of experiencing God's glory! - Romans 5:1-2 TPT

Throughout his journey he faced many challenges. He was beaten, stoned, imprisoned, and shipwrecked multiple times – along with assassination attempts against his life. He faced persecution from every angle. Even some Christians refused to show him forgiveness.

Instead of persecuting Christians, Paul was called to be persecuted as one of them. Can you imagine the nightmares and pain that would come with the kind of past

Paul left behind. He was continually faced with opposition and criticism. He had memories that he couldn't erase. He had to deal with the decisions he once made. He not only faced the challenges of the world against him, but he also had to face the internal battle within himself.

In his early life before the encounter, Paul had a hardened heart. He was prideful and arrogant. He harbored anger and hate. He hunted down Christians. It is not certain if he was directly involved in murdering followers of Jesus, but scripture tells us he did approve the imprisonment and murder of them.

When you look at the life of Paul and all that he was set free from – you can see a beautiful picture of God's miraculous power and grace! He needed that grace! Without such great understanding of grace, he would not have weathered the trials.

From the moment Paul became a believer in Christ, His life was transformed. He was given a new identity and new purpose that redefined his life.

He was so convinced of the grace of God that even after being in isolated dark prison cells he could say things like –

I can do all things (which He has called me to do] through Him who strengthens and empowers me [to fulfill His purpose—I am self-sufficient in Christ's sufficiency; I am ready for anything and equal to anything

through Him who infuses me with inner
strength and confident peace.)
- Philippians 4:13 AMP

Despite never witnessing Jesus' ministry, Paul arguably
contributed more to the growth of the Christian movement
than any other apostle. He laid the foundation for missions
work that has continued around the world today, and
through his life he modeled evangelism, discipleship,
perseverance, and suffering—for the Christians who knew
him, and for every believer living today.

And the most powerful truth in the story of Paul is this:

It was God's Grace that saved him!

It was by Grace he was forgiven!

It was *Grace Over Guilt* that forever changed him!

Imagine this - the day Paul entered Heaven he was
welcomed in by the applause and the cheers of the men,
women, and children he persecuted!

That's the Gospel!

[The story of Paul written in chapter twelve "Grace over Guilt" is from, Who Was the Apostle Paul? by Ryan Nelson | Feb 28, 2019, overviewbible.com]

Cover layout by Jenn@fosterchic - fiverr.com / eliteonlinepublishing.com

Written by Armando Perez - APerezbooks@outlook.com